RECOVERING
from
NARCISSISTIC
MOTHERS

RECOVERING
from
NARCISSISTIC
MOTHERS

A DAUGHTER'S GUIDE

Brenda Stephens, LPCC

ROCKRIDGE
PRESS

For general information on our other products and services or to obtain technical support, please contact our Customer Care Department within the United States at (866) 744-2665, or outside the United States at (510) 253-0500.

Rockridge Press publishes its books in a variety of electronic and print formats. Some content that appears in print may not be available in electronic books, and vice versa.

Interior and Cover Designer: Stephanie Sumulong
Art Producer: Samantha Ulban
Editor: Shannon Criss
Production Editor: Nora Milman and Ruth Sakata Corley

All images used under license iStock.
Author photo courtesy of Julia Glover.

ISBN: Print 978-1-64739-713-5 | eBook 978-1-64739-714-2
R0

*To those seeking recovery
from narcissistic abuse,
and to my own mother.
Your courage is inspiring.*

Contents

Introduction

When Erika began therapy, she wrote quite a bit more on her intake form than most of my clients do. I was grateful for the information while also appalled by some of what she shared about her mother. What I read described a lack of boundaries, enmeshment, and control this mother tried to enforce over her daughter, who was now a young adult. It all led to a level of anxiety, depression, and panic that consumed Erika's life. Erika had seen a few therapists in the past, but the insidiousness of narcissistic abuse did not seem to be something these therapists understood. Few therapists recognize this type of abuse and how it differs from more overt types of abuse such as physical violence or neglect. The abuse children experience from a narcissistic mother is subtle and mostly invisible to everyone else. The child, however, feels it at their core and builds defenses early on to protect themselves from the emotional torment a narcissistic parent inflicts on the trusting, validation-seeking child.

My name is Brenda Stephens, and I have been a licensed professional clinical counselor for several years. Over the span of my career, I started to notice a similar theme with some of my clients who were seeking therapy. The common phrase I kept hearing was "am I crazy, or …?" My clients were lost in their own perceptions of their lives. They had been gaslighted by the person who was supposed to love, nurture, and care for them and validate their experiences and emotions. As adults, they had entered relationships that were also dysfunctional. Noticing a pattern, these people approached therapy with guilt and the belief that they were the problem since nearly all of their relationships were unhealthy.

I strongly encourage those reading this book to seek out therapy, psychiatric care, support groups, or other resources to help navigate your recovery process. There are a growing number of mental health providers who are starting to recognize and treat the victims of this unique and insidious type of abuse, so there are professionals who *get it*. Most mental health providers want to make sure they're the right fit for you, so don't be afraid to ask prospective providers if they understand this type of abuse in order to find the right person to guide you through your journey.

In this book, you will find stories and anecdotes you will likely relate to and find eerily familiar. In my practice, I see that the nature of narcissistic abuse is surprisingly consistent. I often tell clients that it is almost as if narcissists have an abuse playbook they all share. You'll also see that the reactions, responses, and pain of the abused are strikingly common as well.

I hope you will see that you are not alone. By the end of this book, you will be better equipped to identify what narcissistic abuse is, how it has affected so many areas of your life, and most importantly, how you can recover and create and maintain healthy, nurturing relationships moving forward. You will gain a deeper understanding of narcissistic personality disorder and what causes this disorder. You will learn how to navigate communication to protect yourself from the manipulation you have experienced with a narcissistic mother. You will also learn the most important defense tactic to use with a narcissist: the creation and maintenance of boundaries.

How This Book Can Help

This book is separated into two parts. The first part will enhance your understanding of what narcissistic personality disorder is and how it develops. You will see that although the diagnosable disorder has stringent criteria to meet, narcissism can run on a continuum. Understanding this disorder will help you recognize that you are not who or what you believed yourself to be through the lens of the narcissist. You will see that there are different types of narcissists and not all of them fit into the diagnostic mold that we see in clinical books and practice. In learning about the causes of narcissistic personality disorder, you may gain compassion and empathy for the narcissist, since they typically develop this disorder due to their own experiences with trauma. Having compassion and empathy does not excuse the behavior, but it does allow you to be true to yourself. More important, it will help you understand that the abuse was never an indicator of your worth. Rather, it is evidence of how wounded the abuser feels.

You have the power to reclaim your identity and learn about who you are at your core. Self-love and self-care will become important to you as you start to see your own value. You will gain an understanding of the importance of validation and how daughters of narcissistic mothers spend so much of their time seeking this validation without finding a way to fill the emptiness. You will see that it is possible to build self-esteem and essentially parent yourself to provide the validation, nurturing, and love that you have always craved. The exercises, stories, and anecdotes will help you recognize what parental narcissistic abuse is and how it has affected you throughout your life.

This is hard work and it will take time. You will begin to emerge as a version of yourself that you have never seen before but who lives within you already. There are no quick fixes in this process, but as you move through your journey to recovery, you will notice small changes. When you start to nurture your core self, you will realize it is no longer acceptable to use disparaging language toward yourself. You will show yourself the respect and kindness that you so freely show to others.

RECOGNIZING THE NARCISSISTIC MOTHER

How do you recognize narcissism in your mother? Do you have enough objectivity to come to this conclusion, or are you too close? This section will provide insight into the characteristics of narcissists and the different types of narcissism that exist. Armed with this information, you will be better equipped to identify narcissism.

In part one, we will look at research and theories of how narcissism develops in individuals and how it affects parenting. We will focus on how being the daughter of a narcissist can lead you to doubt your worth and create feelings of never being good enough. We will also explore how daughters of narcissistic mothers tend to seek validation through achievement but never seem to achieve enough to fill the void. Self-sabotage, hypervigilance, anxiety, low stress tolerance, and low self-esteem haunt daughters of narcissists no matter how successful they may be in their careers or in their personal lives. Self-doubt can be all-consuming, tainting the positive in the daughter's life and leading her to credit other circumstances for her own successes. Understanding the causes of narcissistic personality disorder and its increased prevalence in our society will decrease the mystery behind this disorder.

CHAPTER ONE

What Is Narcissistic Personality Disorder?

In Greek mythology, Narcissus was a figure who was incredibly handsome. Because he was so vain, he rebuffed those who admired him. After he broke one too many hearts, a goddess cursed him to fall in love with himself. He came upon his reflection in a pond and would not leave the water. At each attempt he made to drink from the pool, his reflection would disappear, so he withered away as he sat gazing at himself. It is from this myth that the modern sense of narcissism is derived.

The fifth edition of the *Diagnostic and Statistical Manual of Mental Disorders*, or the *DSM-5*, describes narcissistic personality disorder as "a grandiose sense of self-importance. A preoccupation with fantasies of unlimited success, power, brilliance, beauty, or ideal love. A belief that he or she is special and unique and can only be understood by, or should only associate with, other special or high-status people or institutions. A need for excessive admiration." When we understand where this disorder stems from, we understand that when the narcissist is cruel, she is showing how emotionally destroyed she is. The narcissist attacks others because of her own pain. Knowing this, you will see that you don't have to believe the cruel words she is saying to you. This is the first step in the journey toward recovery.

Causes of NPD

While it's not fully understood how this disorder develops, it is likely a combination of environment, genetics, and the way the brain is wired. Some narcissists develop this disorder by being overly praised by parents who have tried to fuel their own self-esteem through the achievements of their children. In therapy, clinicians often see narcissistic personality disorder resulting from neglect and abuse during childhood. Often, the child has been shown that they are not important and their needs are not a priority. As they grow older, they overcompensate for this treatment and rely on the attention and validation of others to create a version of themselves that will be desirable to others. No matter the cause, the consistent result is that the narcissist goes on to create unhealthy and abusive relationships. Below, we will focus on possible contributors to this disorder.

Insensitive Parenting

A neglectful or indifferent parent is certain to create an unhealthy and non-nurturing environment in which a child can't thrive. The exact way that this parental dysfunction shows up in children is not fully known. However, children who grow up neglected often have a hard time functioning when they're emotionally overwhelmed. Neglected children may lack self-identity. These children spend most of their time trying to figure out how to stay in the good graces of their neglectful parent and receive any attention that they can, be it good or bad. Neglected children are forced to act as their own parents—becoming "parentified"—because they are left with the responsibility of meeting their own needs.

Parentified children miss out on childhood and feel discarded. When they reach adulthood, they often lack a strong sense of self because they spent so much time and energy focusing on trying to survive an unhealthy dynamic with their parents. Parental neglect frequently leads to deep feelings of self-doubt. Without the attention they need at home, the neglected child seeks the adoration and validation of others to feel whole. Children learn empathy through the relationships they have in childhood, starting with their parents. When they aren't receiving validation and compassion from caregivers, they don't know what empathy is or how to have empathy for others.

Excessive Praise or Pampering

My first thought when considering this pathway to narcissism is of Cinderella's stepsisters. Their mother saw them as an extension of herself and gave them praise they did not deserve. She taught them to be superficial and only concerned for themselves. She taught them to use people and discard them when they no longer needed them. This is a less common path to narcissism, but it does take place. Children first learn from caregivers, usually parents, and they are little sponges sopping up everything they hear and see. If a child is told how special she is, the child will likely believe this. When a parent does not let a child learn the consequences of their behavior or the value of earning a privilege, they are creating a person who thinks everyone else is less valuable. As the child develops, they will believe that those less fortunate have created their own circumstances and that there are only select others who are worth their time, looking down on the rest. No matter which path leads to narcissism, two of its hallmarks are a lack of empathy and an exaggerated sense of superiority, accompanied by the belief that only other superior people are worthy of attention.

Excessive Criticism

It may seem counterintuitive to think that excessive criticism might lead to narcissistic traits, but the human brain is always trying to find balance. Therefore, if a child grows up with an excessively critical caretaker, the child's self-talk as she is developing will be language that challenges and counteracts the criticism. She will over-compensate in trying to prove to herself and to her parents that she has value. This constant criticism will leave her struggling to understand who she is at her core. She believes the negative words and messages she has received from her caregiver, and to prove to herself that she is capable, she likely overachieves.

Sadly, criticism ultimately wins. The developing child is caught in a war within herself trying to believe that she is more worthwhile than she has been told she is while also believing that she is not good enough. Excessive criticism is damaging for anyone, and a child is not equipped to manage the emotional fallout that comes from consistently being told that they are not measuring up. Excessive criticism of a child can hamper her ability to adapt to change and function well when she's feeling emotional.

Trauma

You may start noticing a theme here as we talk about trauma. In my work, the trauma I most consistently see is complex trauma, which is a result of long-term exposure to abuse, undeserved blame, and witnessing the mistreatment of others, usually a family member. In abusive families, children are often left to fend for themselves. Even when there are peaceful times, the child cannot relax because they are waiting for the next round of chaos or the next threat. They become hypervigilant and are not able to let their guard down. They don't connect well with other family members, especially the siblings they're competing with for attention and sometimes for basic necessities like food. Abuse undermines a person's sense of self-worth. Abuse tells the victim that they have little value and are a burden to the abuser. The child, again, does not develop a sense of identity, ego strength, or self-esteem when raised in this type of environment. As they mature, they can start to develop narcissistic traits because they have to look for validation from others. Their lifeblood is the admiration others provide, commonly referred to as "supply."

Extremely High Expectations

This path to narcissism is not totally distinct from excessive criticism, but it is worth mentioning. The path involves a parent who sees their child as an extension of themselves and takes the child's failures as their own, therefore creating expectations that don't allow room for mistakes or failure. This could lead to narcissistic traits in a couple of ways. The child may be able to reach the expectations of the parent, but she'll exert so much energy on doing so that she doesn't have time to figure out who she is or what is important to her. Her sense of self is only defined by achievement. Because this is the only value she has, she is left with a personality that consists entirely of being the best at everything she attempts, and she will devalue things that she is not successful at and people who do not recognize how special she is. Another way high expectations can lead to narcissism is when the child is not able to meet those expectations and has to create her own reality in which she is superior in other ways.

Gene Abnormality

There is so much that we don't know about how the brain works. For many years, personality disorders have been attributed to poor skills in managing emotions and navigating relationships. There is increasing evidence that there are some neurological influences on personality disorders, including narcissism.

According to a study by Kamila Jankowiak-Siuda and Wojciech Zajkowski published in the *Medical Science Monitor*, "in the affective domain, empathy is often understood as the ability to share and co-experience the feelings of others. From the cognitive perspective, empathy is the ability to imagine and understand the emotions and motives of others and the ability to be consciously aware of their thoughts, intentions, and desires, which is known as mentalizing or having a theory of mind." They explain that brain scans of some people with narcissism show faulty connections in the area where some empathetic responses are processed. Deficits in this part of the brain could lead a person to focus on the self rather than on others. Low empathy is a fundamental characteristic of narcissists.

A NARCISSISTIC SOCIETY

According to an article published in the *Journal of Clinical Psychiatry*, the prevalence of narcissistic personality disorder in the United States is approximately 6 percent. The study reported that the rate is higher for men (7.7 percent) than it is for women (4.8 percent).

As mentioned previously, there is not enough research on the genetic or environmental causes of narcissism, partially because we don't typically see narcissists in clinical settings asking for assistance. Notably, the structures of society are still set up in a way that can encourage and reward narcissistic traits. Men and women—but especially men—tend to get further in life when they exhibit confidence and assertiveness. Additionally, social media and consumerism can influence how we see ourselves and what we value. We start to believe that the key to feeling adequate is to drive the best car, have the best job, and be the most attractive. We've learned to value the superficial, which validates narcissistic behavior by making it more acceptable to ignore empathy and focus on the self.

We hear the word "narcissist" being tossed around casually because we currently exist in a society that, in many ways, encourages and fosters narcissism. Social media and consumerism contribute to the objectification of women in particular, producing a cycle of rewarding superficial behavior while disregarding the actual person..

Identifying NPD

The *DSM-5* explains that five of the following criteria should be met in order to diagnose narcissistic personality disorder:

→ Grandiose sense of self
→ Fixation on fantasies of success, control, brilliance, beauty, or ideal love
→ Belief that they are extraordinary and can only be understood by, or should connect with, other extraordinary people
→ Desire for unwarranted admiration
→ Sense of entitlement
→ Interpersonally oppressive behavior
→ Lack of empathy
→ Envy of others or a belief that others are envious of them
→ Arrogant or haughty behavior—conceited, boastful, and pretentious

Many clinicians see narcissism on a continuum. What we see are people who range from having some traits of narcissism to the full-blown disorder. We all have narcissistic traits; it's only when these traits consistently present a problem in everyday functioning that they are considered a clinical issue. Let's explore what this looks like.

The narcissist is an opportunist. Because narcissists tend to lack empathy and often exhibit interpersonally oppressive behavior, it is typical for any narcissist to take advantage of those around them and use others to advance their own interests. They will easily twist facts to make their behavior seem reasonable and maybe even convince their victim that acquiescing to the narcissist's wishes is in their best interest. This is cold and uncaring behavior in any relationship, but when a mother does this to her own child it is especially unacceptable. The power differential already exists in a parent-child relationship, so the influence and expectations of the parent are significant.

A narcissistic mother will not have the empathy to feel for her child when she uses her child for her own needs. This often manifests in a narcissistic mother's relationship with her daughter as an enmeshed relationship. The mother has no boundaries with her daughter and burdens her with the emotional turmoil and low self-worth the mother feels (but would never admit). The mother will use her daughter, whom she sees as an extension of herself, to build her own ego. She will manipulate her daughter into showering her with praise and doing her bidding.

The narcissist is disconnected from reality. When we think of narcissists, we typically think of haughtiness, a sense of entitlement, and an inflated sense of self-importance. What is not spoken about often enough is the delusional thinking that is common among narcissists. A narcissistic mother typically lives in a world that she creates in her mind. She is lost in a fantasy, and she has convinced herself that her expansive dreams and beliefs about herself are true. She will often get involved in many projects or activities to work toward this idealized version of herself, then give up on them when they don't happen quickly enough.

On the surface, this may not seem destructive, but when the narcissistic mother takes her daughter on this trip through her fantasies of her ideal self, the daughter loses her own drive and only focuses on her mother. The daughter often becomes parentified in this dynamic, because mom will crash from her delusional high and the daughter will be expected to pick up the pieces and reassure mom that she is still as wonderful as she thinks she is. The daughter is disregarded in both the rise and the fall of mom's dreams, and her mother doesn't even notice.

The narcissist is manipulative. This trait is a hallmark of the narcissist and is a baseline from which they all seem to operate. Being manipulative is something that we are all guilty of at times. You might have had experiences with manipulation from people who may not matter much to you. A salesperson might try to persuade you to buy the more expensive item so they get a higher commission, or a political canvasser may try to convince you that the candidate you prefer is a poor choice by twisting facts in their candidate's favor. These are annoying but don't tend to have an emotional effect on you.

When someone who has an authority position or an emotional connection to you manipulates you, it strikes a much more vulnerable part of you. A mother will know how to push buttons and gain sympathy from you in a way that most people wouldn't be aware of. She has studied you since you were born, and she is in a prime position to manipulate you because she knows you so well. She will use shame and guilt to control you and enlist you in getting what she needs. She will work on your sympathy and your sense of duty to her. She will also harshly criticize you for any resistance to her agenda.

The narcissist is envious. As you now know, narcissism often develops as a result of abuse and/or neglect. When a parent has no regard and sees no value in their child, that child is left with a deep sense of emptiness. The child tries to fill that void by gaining material items and by seeking attention and validation from others. As they develop and mature, the narcissist sees wealth, beauty, popularity, and social status as something they deserve. If they don't have these things, they obsess over it. Envy can be very ugly, and it's even uglier when it is coming from a mother toward her daughter. This is one of the more insidious behaviors of a narcissistic mother. Instead of fulfilling her role as a nurturer, she is a destructive force in her daughter's life. A mother can be envious of her daughter's beauty, youth, success, or any other quality and work diligently to convince her daughter that she owes all the credit to her mother. She will manipulate her daughter into believing that she has no qualities of her own and has gotten everything through pure luck, or she might convince her daughter that her achievements are not worthwhile.

The narcissist has a superiority complex. Narcissists have spent their lives trying to convince themselves that they have worth; by doing so, they convince themselves that they are superior to nearly everyone. She will try to be the smartest, wealthiest, and most beautiful person in the room. Any attention she gets is confirmation of her superiority and gives her the supply of admiration that fuels her. This supply is what keeps the narcissist thriving, and she will do whatever she has to in order to get it.

Whenever narcissists do not feel like they are the most superior person in a given situation, they will often try to align with the person they see filling this role. The narcissist will disregard others, even her own daughter, if it gains her access to the person she is idolizing who can bring her own sense of value higher. We don't speak much about how a narcissist tries to make these connections to increase their own worth, but it is quite common and so damaging for a daughter to see her mother working hard to connect with someone else while treating her daughter with such disdain.

The narcissist is pretentious. Pretentiousness is closely related to the narcissist's superiority complex. After all that time spent convincing themselves that they have worth, the narcissist now needs to convince others so that their supply of attention and admiration will continue. The narcissist will go to great lengths to show their importance, such as bribing officials to let their children into their prestigious school so that the narcissistic mother can boast about this (imagine what this does to the self-worth of the daughter of a narcissist). The narcissist will live above her means to show off her wealth. She will wear the best clothes and live in the best neighborhoods, and she will make sure her children go to the best schools. When she can't afford these things, she will go into debt without hesitation to brag about her successes. Her daughter will see the ugly side: she will see that her mother has scammed the landlord to live in the fancy house or gotten a housekeeping job on the yacht so that she can brag to her unknowing friends that she spent yet another day cruising the ocean. It's all an illusion.

The narcissist is materialistic. The theme of superficiality continues with this trait. The narcissistic mother thinks that having items with a high price tag and a designer label will fill that feeling of emptiness she can't shake. She does whatever she can to gain items of value and starts to believe that they reflect *her* true value. As noted above, she is a master at twisting the truth and manipulating circumstances in her favor. She spends much of her energy and her time trying to feel whole, and she thrives on the satisfaction she feels when trying on that new designer dress and wearing it out to dinner. As that dress hangs in the closet at the end of the day, the void reappears, and she cannot tolerate it. She cannot sit with feelings of emptiness and be forced to explore why she feels depressed, lonely, and worthless. She needs another distraction, so she gets on her computer to research the most luxurious car she can find. This will hold her over until she can go to the lot tomorrow for a test drive. The satisfaction of gaining objects is fleeting, and thus this is a never-ending cycle.

The narcissist lacks empathy. Empathy is hard to identify, but we know it when we feel it. We believe we can see it expressed by others. There are examples of empathy around us every day, and it really is key to a cohesive society. Thus, a lack of empathy is very difficult for us to understand. When clients sit in session with me and talk about a loved one, they will describe moments when they believe they witnessed empathy coming from their narcissist. A daughter will be convinced that when her mother shed a tear for that lonely kid in a movie they watched together, her mother showed empathy. The more likely reason behind that tear was that her mother had a moment of recognition of her own childhood and felt sorrow for her child self, not for the child in the movie. This can be a hard construct for the daughter to come to terms with, as she so strongly wants to believe that her mother is a kind, loving woman. A difficult part of the journey for the daughter is realizing that her mother is not who she thought she was.

QUIZ:
DOES YOUR MOTHER EXHIBIT NARCISSISTIC TRAITS?

Check the box next to each question that resonates with you.

☐ Does your mother seem like a different person to you in public settings?

☐ Does she harshly criticize you for the way you look?

☐ Did she pay an unhealthy amount of attention to the way your body looked?

☐ Does it feel like she is competing with you?

☐ Does she seem engaged and warm one day and distant and cold the next?

☐ Did she fail to support your interests and show up for you, then turn around and brag about you if you did well?

☐ Did she question how much money you spent on things you wanted?

☐ Did she make grand gestures that were supposed to celebrate you, then steal the spotlight for herself?

☐ Did she shame you for engaging in typical age-appropriate behaviors as you were growing up?

Remember that narcissism often runs on a continuum and is more extreme in some cases than others. This quiz might help you see where your mother falls on this range, although of course only a licensed therapist can give a formal diagnosis of a personality disorder. All of these questions relate back to the traits previously noted in this chapter, and it is a good exercise to match them up to your own experiences. You can see how the mother can often see the daughter as an extension of herself, so her criticisms of her daughter are often a projection of how much she dislikes herself.

Donna Attempts to Please Her Mother

A previous client of mine, Donna, was the daughter of a refugee mother. Donna's mother was rather old-fashioned in her idea of womanhood, and she dressed to impress every day whether she left the house or not. She expected Donna to follow in her footsteps in order to be an acceptable representation of her mother, which Donna dutifully did throughout her adolescence.

Donna's mother beamed with pride when Donna met and married a wealthy man and moved to a coveted neighborhood, but her mother's expectations only got higher and she put more pressure on Donna to wear the right clothes, drive the right car, and never make a spectacle of herself so that she could fit in with the other high-class women in the neighborhood. As time passed, Donna became increasingly miserable in her marriage and started to suspect that her husband was also a narcissist. She felt validated when she learned that many of us try to correct past relationships with new ones and often end up with the same type of person who hurt us in the past.

As her marriage began to crumble, Donna's husband isolated her and started a smear campaign against her with their once-mutual friends. Donna was crushed by the end of her marriage and the fact that her children had also turned against her. She had no one left to turn to but her mother. She was forced to move back in with her, and the abuse started all over again.

Donna's mother insisted that Donna do whatever it took to return to her husband despite the fact that Donna had been completely broken by the relationship. Donna's mother presented what she thought were compelling reasons for Donna to get back together with her ex. She would pose superficial questions: Where would the extended family go for Christmas this year? Who would make sure the children stayed connected to the other families in the neighborhood that could help them get into good colleges? Not once did she give Donna a reason to return that would benefit Donna.

When Donna reluctantly tried to reconcile with her husband, she gained her mother's approval. Every time the relationship failed, she was treated with disdain. Donna became more and more depressed, which caused physical ailments to surface. But each time Donna made an appointment with her doctor to treat these concerns, her mother suddenly became ill and Donna would have to cancel her own appointments to tend to her mother's health. Their relationship was toxic.

As you can see from this example, the effects of having a narcissistic mother do not stop when the daughter reaches adulthood. There are many reasons a daughter maintains the relationship and, sadly, continues to be subjected to the abuse. In my practice, I'll hear clients justify keeping their mothers in their lives, saying things like, "Well, she's my mother and I have no choice," or "She can be sweet sometimes." The sense of obligation to our parents is instilled in all of us on a societal level. That obligation is drilled into us even further by the manipulations of a narcissistic mother who uses guilt, shame, and even helplessness to get her needs met. The mother will get her needs met even if it ultimately makes her look weak or foolish. The need for attention and adoration is like a drug the narcissist cannot live without. If she doesn't get this attention and adoration, her narcissistic mask falls off as she faces the pain and emptiness she feels in her core.

Donna experienced her mother's insatiable need for status and attention in different ways, which is common in these relationships. Donna was used as an extension of her mother even as she entered adulthood. Donna's mother had control over her, and in return, Donna did whatever her mother wanted her to do so that she could maintain their relationship. The emotional turmoil of Donna's divorce and the upheaval of appeasing her mother made Donna so exhausted and ill that she could no longer function. She spent days on end in bed and could not muster the energy to interact with her mother, even though they lived together and she had nowhere else to go. Her mother could not stand the isolation from her main source of narcissistic supply, so she played the victim. She relied on her daughter's sense of duty, empathy, compassion, and even pity to get the attention she desperately needed.

Donna lost everything, her health deteriorated, her children and friends would not speak to her due to her husband's smear campaign, her depression was crippling, and she retreated deeper into the den of her mother's abuse out of desperation. But she started to see the truth of her relationship with her mother. Donna informally diagnosed her mother with narcissistic personality disorder after doing research on the presentation and diagnostic criteria.

The disorder should only be diagnosed by a mental health professional, but that is often impossible. It's rare for narcissists to seek therapy because they will not admit there is anything wrong with them. When therapists see narcissists in the therapy room, it is often because they come with a partner. Couples counseling does not tend to last long after the narcissist realizes they cannot manipulate the therapist. Narcissists are sometimes ordered to go to therapy by a judge, either as part of a divorce proceeding or because they've ended up on the wrong side of the law. But as you might imagine, narcissists who are forced to go to therapy do not typically get much out of the experience.

Narcissistic Profiles

It helps to understand that there are different types of narcissists and that your mother likely fits one profile more than the others. The more knowledge you have about where your mother's motives stem from, the easier it will be for you to create your boundaries. Narcissistic behavior can be very subtle, and when the narcissist in your life is your own mother, she has the power advantage in some significant ways. She's been telling you stories about herself for your entire life, and it can be hard to sort out what's true. More information will make you better prepared to defend yourself. For example, if your mother is a "communal narcissist," it can be confusing when you see her doing good deeds and getting praise because you also see the side of her that is cruel and abusive. Understanding the different types of narcissistic personalities will help to clear the fog that comes with your relationship with your mother.

Communal Narcissist

Narcissism can be complicated and confusing. "Communal narcissist" is surely an oxymoron, right? How can someone be so absorbed with herself and be concerned about her community?

It all boils down to motive. All narcissists have manipulative tendencies, but the sneakiness of the communal narcissist is in a league of its own. I've worked with a lot of clients over the years who come from differing backgrounds and have narcissistic parents with jobs that ranged from landscaping to brain surgery. What bands communal narcissist parents together is the behavior within these careers: they use their position in the world to do good deeds in order to feed their narcissistic urges.

The clearest example is narcissistic pastors. I cannot think of a better career for the shattered narcissist than being the head of a church; I've had three clients who are the daughters of narcissistic pastors. That career can feed the narcissistic supply in so many ways. As a pastor, the narcissist always has control and adoration. Top that off with the unconditional love that abounds in her faith, and she's got it made! Add social media to the mix, and the narcissistic mother has affirmation and validation and a platform that has the potential to reach untold numbers of people. Anytime she's out doing good deeds in the community, it's a win: she is shown gratitude, acceptance, and adoration, and she is even emulated by parishioners who try to follow her lead.

Covert Narcissist

The covert narcissist is one of the hardest types of narcissist to recognize. A person who shows up and must tell you how much they spent on the new Rolex on their wrist is easy to spot. However, the person who backs you into a corner at a party to tell you all the details of the car crash they were in is less identifiable as a narcissist. The covert narcissist subtly thrives on admiration. They might "accidentally" leave that piece of mail on the counter for you to see the fancy job offer they received, then act humble while you praise them. If you happen to not notice that letter, they will somehow bring it to your attention and then blame you for not noticing things that are important to them. They will reluctantly give you compliments in order to receive them in return, and their compliment to you will be conditional or backhanded: "You would be so pretty if you wore more makeup" or "I always got As in school but it's good that you got that B on your test."

We don't typically expect the narcissist to play the victim, but the covert narcissist does, skillfully. They need attention, so they tell you about how they fell from a ladder and hurt their back (but of course, they were on that ladder to rescue a poor little kitten in the tree for a little old lady).

Malignant Narcissist

This is the most toxic narcissist there is—and the most obvious. They may be the narcissists who were most wounded in childhood and have the least amount of empathy. This type of narcissist is controlling, paranoid, and cruel. When my client Donna finally moved out of her mother's home, her mother insisted on keeping one of Donna's cardboard boxes. When Donna asked her mother what she wanted the box for, her mother replied, "It's a good size to hide a torso." Donna was shocked at the threatening undertones of this comment, and her mother immediately claimed it was a joke.

On more than one occasion, I have had clients whose phones buzzed incessantly through our session. These clients will typically know what to expect and when they finally check their phone and are not surprised that their narcissist has texted them 148 times over the course of a 50-minute session. The narcissist cannot stand not knowing where her source of supply is and will do everything in her power to get them back.

The malignant narcissist rages and can become violent, but she will always blame her victim for "making me act this way." A malignant narcissist mother will say cruel and vile things to her daughter and then expect forgiveness when she needs supply. She'll give a "fauxpology" while dodging responsibility for her behavior, saying something like, "I'm sorry you made me so mad that I lost control."

MYTH: Social media turns people into narcissists. In fact, social media is not responsible for turning people into narcissists, but it does give them an easy platform from which to gain more attention.

MYTH: All narcissists are outgoing. We expect a narcissist to be jovial and outgoing, but this is not always true. Just because someone has a quiet demeanor doesn't mean they can't be a narcissist. When someone drains your energy, it's time to look at why. When they make you feel like your brain is in a fog or like you're "going crazy," pay attention. Your intuition is telling you something that your brain is ignoring.

MYTH: All narcissists have low self-esteem. This is a little controversial. Some will say this is true, but others say it's false. I believe the confusion lies in the presentation. Considering that there is not a healthy path to personality disordered traits, this is inherently true to some degree.

MYTH: People with narcissistic personality disorder can have healthy relationships. Given that one of the hallmarks of NPD is lack of empathy, this is not true. You must care about others to have healthy relationships. Period.

MYTH: You can change a narcissist. This false hope is why so many of us stay loyal to our narcissists for so long. We hope they will change. We hope that our mothers will finally apologize for the hurt they have caused us and then we will feel whole. They don't change.

The Narcissistic Mother's Artillery

Daughters of narcissistic mothers are wounded to the core. Their own emotional development is stunted. These daughters are forced to either exist in a hypervigilant state waiting for the next round of chaos, or to make themselves invisible to avoid being the target of their mother's abuse. They learn to not trust their own decisions and often find themselves in codependent relationships as adults. The daughter does not have the opportunity to develop her own sense of identity and feels hopelessly lost once she reaches adulthood and finds herself in another relationship in which the other person takes control. The daughter may have been criticized to the point of developing panic attacks, eating disorders, and migraines. When we don't learn to identify our emotions and have them validated by caregivers, our emotional development is hindered. Let's look at the narcissistic mother's weapons of choice.

Lack of Boundaries

To a narcissist, another person's boundaries are a barrier to the control they wish to have. Because of the built-in power imbalance, a narcissistic mother feels she has no rules to follow when it comes to her daughter. There are no secrets, and there are no questions too personal for the mother to ask. The daughter has no privacy, so she learns to hide who she is. She acquiesces to her mother's every demand because it is easier than facing the rage if she doesn't.

The level of control a narcissistic mother expects to have over her daughter is devastating to the daughter. The mother is oppressive, and if she can remove all barriers to control, she will have complete access to the narcissistic supply she needs. If the mother essentially creates a daughter who always goes along with whatever she needs, the mother has her most important drug: constant attention and validation.

The lack of boundaries leads to an enmeshed relationship between mother and daughter where their roles are often blurred. In an enmeshed mother-daughter relationship, the daughter can be treated as a friend; sometimes the daughter even acts as a parent to make the mother feel needed and cared for. The daughter can be exposed at a young age to adult information and situations that she does not have the emotional capacity to manage. This robs the daughter of a childhood. The daughter is unable to be carefree and cared for as every child deserves.

Toxic Shame

The root of so many psychological issues is shame. We all feel shame from time to time, and it can be a helpful emotion in making sure societal norms are adhered to. It's when shame becomes a state of being that it becomes toxic.

The narcissistic mother will shame her child tactically so that the child will put her mother first and obey her every demand in order to avoid more shame. What better way to have complete control over another person than getting them to the point where they have shame for simply existing? The narcissistic mother is a master at creating toxic shame. She has time and motive to chip away at her daughter's opinions, ideas, confidence, and identity. Once the narcissistic mother does this, she has all the power. The daughter is paralyzed with fear of being exposed, so she does whatever is expected of her by her mother.

Shame is so internalized by children that it can become a baseline from which they function. Shame also creates other challenges and struggles such as chronic anxiety, depression, and low self-esteem. A daughter who's been systematically shamed will often be very impressionable since she has been taught not to trust herself. Shame can lead to rebellion in the daughter, although she will not likely lash out at her mother as that is too dangerous. She will generally turn that rebellion inward by engaging in self-harm or substance abuse to escape the way she feels about herself. When she's stuck in this pattern, the daughter cannot win.

Control

Throughout this chapter, we have seen what an integral part control plays in narcissism. Control is an umbrella trait of narcissism: all the behaviors of the narcissist have some root in control. Having control means no surprises and no concerns that the narcissistic mask will slip and the vulnerable person behind it will be exposed. Control means that the narcissistic mother has her supply available to her whenever she needs a fix.

The narcissist needs to be in control to avoid narcissistic injury, which is a motivating factor for all the behaviors the narcissist exhibits. The *DSM-5* says that narcissists exhibit "vulnerability in self-esteem, which makes narcissistic people very sensitive to 'injury' from criticism or defeat. Although they may not show it outwardly, criticism may haunt these individuals and may leave them feeling humiliated, degraded, hollow, and empty. They react with disdain, rage, or defiant counterattack."

A narcissistic mother will have no shame in how she gains control because her daughter is essentially a captive audience. She can behave outrageously without risk of losing the relationship, because the daughter is too young for independence and eventually just sees this as normal. It is so disturbing for the daughter to see her mother in this state that she will do her best to ensure it won't happen again.

Competition

The narcissist is in a perpetual state of trying to prove her worth, mostly to herself. Competition, even with her own daughter, confirms her belief that she is better than others. She sees proof of her own superiority even when she loses a competition, which is counterintuitive. If she loses, she can easily dismiss this by making some excuse (she wasn't well rested, her daughter cheated, etc.). The results of coming out ahead in competition are more obvious: she will feel superior, which confirms her bias toward herself, even if she wins a sprint from the car to the house when returning from the grocery store. No victory is too small, and she will put her need to win above an opportunity to build her daughter's confidence.

The narcissistic mother likely sees all women as competition, and she cannot value other women because she can see them only as a threat to her worth and probably her beauty. As her daughter matures, she too is a threat, and the narcissistic mother makes sure that she reduces this threat. She overly criticizes her daughter by pointing out her flaws and will even compare her own perfection to her daughter's imperfections. Due to her own beliefs about her worth, she might teach her children that a woman's beauty and fitness are what define her worth, which places unreasonable expectations on her daughter. Her daughter learns that she is inferior and mistakenly believes that she needs to strive to be more like her mother, which perpetuates the cycle.

Emotional Disconnect

All personality disorders have a hint of narcissism to them, and we often see traits of the different types of these disorders among family members. Emotional disconnect from any caregiver could be the foundation for this phenomenon.

When a caregiver is emotionally unavailable, the child is left to learn how to interact with the world around them by themselves. They aren't able to develop skills to connect with others and are left desperate for love, affection, and validation. I cannot stress enough the importance these three things have on the healthy development of a child and even a fully grown adult. We are social animals: babies start mimicking the facial expressions of their caregivers early on to establish bonding. Throughout our lives, we need connection with others to thrive. When a child develops without this emotional connection or has this connection only intermittently, they shrivel instead of thriving.

Intermittent emotional connection is almost worse than consistent disconnect of emotions. With intermittent emotional connection, the mother teaches her daughter that she needs to constantly perform to get the attention she needs. Sometimes it will work and other times it won't, and this creates desperation in the daughter's attempts. She will likely focus on achievements to impress her mother and will never fill the void that disconnection from her mother caused.

If the disconnect is consistent, the child will not thrive and she will generally give up. With consistent disconnection, the child does not have the motive to strive to be seen and will likely seek affirmation and acceptance in unhealthy ways.

Erika Fights for Independence

Remember Erika from the beginning of the chapter? Her mother used her arsenal to oppress and control Erika and to keep her as a closely held source of narcissistic supply. Erika's mother, Linda, a single mother, did not allow Erika to grow and develop in a healthy way. She controlled every aspect of Erika's life and was concerned to the point of paranoia about how the mother-daughter pair would be perceived by others. She saw Erika as only an extension of herself instead of a growing child with opinions and feelings of her own. Linda eventually became a leader of women's ministry in her church and as she gained more recognition and admiration, her expectations of her daughter increased.

Erika had kept her high school boyfriend a secret because she knew her mother would have a terrible reaction, and, as Erika predicted, Linda became enraged when she found out. Linda belittled Erika into believing that her boyfriend was only using her for sex and accused Erika of having sex when she had not. Linda took Erika to a gynecologist to confirm her virginity through a medically inaccurate but still humiliating test. Erika was emotionally destroyed by this and was forced to break up with her boyfriend. She was unable to leave the house because of her mother's need to control her and her own feelings of shame at having disappointed her mother.

Later that year, Erika was accepted by a university in another state, and she believed this was her opportunity for independence and freedom. Then she learned that Linda was moving with her. While Erika was able to live in the dorms during the beginning of her college life, she went home every weekend to the apartment her mother rented near the school. Erika's free time was spent with her mother, who monitored her constantly, often incessantly calling and texting Erika knowing that she was in class.

Erika did find time to meet a young man at school and spent time with him after classes during the week without her mother knowing. Erika was excited, and at first, she enjoyed the attention and affection she received from Herbie. After studying in the library one evening, Herbie offered to walk Erika back to her dorm. As they entered the building, he pushed her into the stairwell and sexually assaulted her. After Erika begged him repeatedly to stop, he finally left her alone. Erika had no one to turn to, so she called her mother. Her mother drove to the school to pick Erika up and spent the entire ride back to the apartment accusing Erika of being a slut and telling her she deserved what happened since she put herself in that situation. She told Erika that the fact that she'd been assaulted brought shame to their small family. Erika received no empathy from her mother and was left to deal with the trauma of the assault on her own.

CHAPTER ONE REVIEW

In this chapter we have explored what a narcissist looks like and how their behaviors affect others. We looked at the traits specific to narcissistic mothers and the indescribable pain they inflict upon their daughters. We focused on what can create NPD and the different pathways of coming to this disorder.

My hope is that by understanding how NPD develops, you will also understand that the way your mother treated you had nothing to do with your own value or worth. When she called you names and insulted you, she was projecting what she hated most about herself. She gave you a window to the pain she hides behind the narcissistic mask she wears. This can help you see her as more vulnerable and allow you to be comfortable with the empathy you may continue to feel for her.

You can see how insidious and subtle this disorder is and how important it is to trust your intuition. When you get that tightness in your stomach at something she says, pay attention and do what you can to protect yourself.

As you move forward, remember:
- → The abuse and neglect you received from your mother was never about you.
- → You can repair how you attach to people.
- → It takes a lot of work and time to recover from narcissistic abuse, but it's possible.
- → You can learn to love yourself.
- → Always trust your intuition. Always.

CHAPTER TWO

Growing Up with an NPD Mother

The mother-daughter relationship is a tricky one to navigate. In typical healthy relationships, it starts out simply enough: a mother gives birth and loves her daughter with every ounce of her soul. As her daughter grows, she is there to cuddle her, teach her, provide a sense of safety for her, and validate her. When her daughter enters puberty, it's mom's job to accept, love, and encourage her daughter as she navigates this phase of development. A healthy mother loves her daughter through both good and difficult times, always being a source of support. This is crucial for a growing child as she learns who is she is by what is mirrored through a healthy relationship with her mom. Daughters also learn how to have other relationships through their parents. At a young age, daughters are sponges, soaking up their mother's interactions and learning how to make their own way in the world. When daughters are raised in a loving, compassionate environment, they are more likely to become healthy, independent adults who know how to respect themselves.

A narcissist's daughter grows up in a home that lacks nurturing, validation, and unconditional love, and she often develops into an adult who does not know who she is. She grows up to be hesitant and lost. She does not have a strong sense of self, and because she has been conditioned to cater to her mother's needs, she will often seek relationships in which she can continue to put others before herself.

The descriptions in this chapter of the relationship between narcissistic mothers and their daughters, and the harm that relationship causes, may make your situation seem hopeless; please do not despair. It's important that you have a clear understanding of this dysfunctional mother-daughter dynamic, so it is described in somewhat stark detail here. But you *can* heal from this trauma, and we will discuss the steps you can take toward healing in part 2.

The Mother–Daughter Relationship

It's obvious that the mother-daughter relationship is pivotal to our development. A typical mother carries you inside her; she nurtures you and guides you through all your important milestones; and she provides a model to her daughter of what it means to be a woman. This is—or should be—a special bond.

Bonding between mother and child begins within the first moments of birth, when the child attaches to her mother and learns to trust. The mother provides consistency, meeting her baby daughter's needs for food, affection, and other forms of care. This bond is crucial as it promotes the connection between brain cells that helps the child learn, emote, and build healthy relationships. Whether children bond with their parent at birth or later, they need this relationship. Without it, children have a much harder time developing a sense of who they are. Neglect and apathy from parents can lead to an increase in mental illness for the child and a lack of motivation to reach developmental milestones and independence. Parental bonding and attachment are essential for a child to have the best shot at growing up strong and vigorous both mentally and physically.

Narcissistic mothers do not bond with their children in the way a healthy mother does. The narcissistic mother will not consistently respond to her crying baby and therefore will not teach her child how to get her basic needs met. What her daughter learns through this inconsistent caretaking is that there is no surefire way to gain mom's attention. Having learned this lesson, the daughter will try anything to be seen and heard. This, as you can imagine, can lead to a contentious relationship between the two.

The daughter is set up to fail because she has picked up unhealthy ways to be recognized by her mother; she is also internalizing the fact that her mother can't be relied on. The daughter of a narcissistic mother has the deck stacked against her from the start. As she gets older and starts to interact with her mother, the daughter does not have the skills or resilience to traverse the complexity of trying to meet her mother's ever-changing expectations. The daughter develops a focus on her mother that makes the daughter lose herself. She tries to stay in her mother's good graces and take the crumbs of any love her mother might toss her way, and this is all the daughter will know of her own identity. Most girls feel nurtured and loved by their mothers, whereas the daughter of a narcissistic mother exists to nurture and love her mother.

WHY NARCISSISTS PROCREATE

The reason a narcissist procreates is to feed her own needs. A narcissistic mother may think that having a child will show all her naysayers that they were wrong about her selfishness and ability to care for others. Once she has a child, the narcissist believes she can show that she is capable of loving someone outside of herself. She may also choose to have a child in an effort to fill the void she has inside herself. To her, a child, specifically her daughter, means that she can heal her own abuse and neglect because she has discovered what it means to love unconditionally. Unfortunately, she won't be able to express this unconditional love because she will resent her daughter, dwelling on what she herself wasn't given as a child.

Mother–Daughter Role Reversal

A common trait that therapists see in daughters of narcissistic mothers is a history of daughters taking the role of emotional caretaker. The daughter puts her own needs aside and shifts the attention onto her mother. The term for this behavior is parentification. If you want to see where your narcissist stopped their emotional development, think about how old she seems when she is raging (common with all narcissists). If you understand that your mother's emotional development was stunted in her childhood, you can begin to recognize why she could not handle calling to make a doctor's appointment for you, nor could she create the structure needed for you to have a bedtime. As a person trapped in a childish state, she would find that many parental caretaking tasks were more responsibility than she could handle.

Because the stunted narcissist has little emotional intelligence and little tolerance for frustration, she will start to confide in her daughter about her fears. She tells her daughter things she should be telling her romantic partner or another adult. Through this process, she becomes enmeshed with her daughter and does not tolerate any boundaries that her daughter may try to create. The narcissistic mother will often put the responsibility of caring for younger children onto her daughter, as the mother does not have the emotional bandwidth to manage the stress that comes with parenting. Her daughter does not get to have her own childhood or develop the skills she needs to grow up and have healthy relationships.

Without exception, I have found that daughters of narcissistic mothers have all dealt with parentification or role reversal. This is a hallmark in the mother-daughter relationship. It's typically a topic that the daughter brings up early on in therapy even when she doesn't recognize the pattern for what it is. A common result of this phenomenon is an adult daughter who lacks joy, playfulness, or a sense of humor.

Codependency

It may seem incongruent to think of narcissists as codependent, but codependence is part of how they operate. The narcissist's ego (a person's sense of self-esteem or self-importance) does not come from within themselves as it does for most of us. A narcissist gains her ego strength from what is reflected to her by others in her life. She relies heavily on their admiration for her own sense of self.

As you've likely seen with your own mother or other people with narcissistic tendencies, a narcissist keeps one or two loyal people in her life and relies heavily on them for admiration. She is usually in tight control of these relationships and expects them to be available to her on a whim. Unfortunately for the narcissist, most people are not willing to show the level of devotion she expects, and those relationships tend to start out intensely and then fizzle out quickly. She may come to call people her "good friends" almost overnight, and then promptly have a dramatic falling out with them. Because of her demanding personality and her fragile emotional state, she is not capable of maintaining many relationships long-term.

People who don't know a narcissist well might look at her and see an independent, outgoing woman who is quick to make friends. However, as her daughter, you see the frantic desperation of your mother arranging her social life so she does not have to sit home alone with her own thoughts. As her daughter, you have likely seen yourself as the last choice in these frantic efforts. If your mother can't find someone to go to brunch with, you are expected to drop everything so that she doesn't have to be alone. The narcissistic mother is dependent on others in a way that is unsustainable except for her loyal few. The person she will generally be most dependent on is her romantic partner, if she has one. This can be particularly cruel, because her high demands on her partner—your other parental figure—will essentially leave you without a reliable parent.

Narcissism and Attachment Theory

Attachment theory was originally developed by psychiatrist John Bowlby and developmental psychologist Mary Ainsworth. Their work was groundbreaking in understanding how babies attach to their caregivers, particularly mothers. Studies have explored this even further and have shown that mothers can become attached to their babies during pregnancy. This process can help prepare women for motherhood. A baby with parents who are responsive to her needs is more securely attached and will learn how to trust others. When a child has a foundation of secure attachment to her parents, then she will be confident that they care for her, and she will be better able to move through the world knowing they will be there to support her. A child whose needs are not met consistently does not learn trust early, nor does she learn how to manage emotions or stress. Attachment styles follow us through life until we do the work required to learn how to have loving, trusting relationships.

Attachment Styles

Luckily, we are not condemned to a life sentence by our attachment style: with perseverance, we can overcome the patterns we learned as babies and children. Unfortunately, we usually go through a few bad relationships before we realize that this is an area of our mental health that needs attention.

Early attachment styles set the stage for the kind of relationships we will have later in life. When you are raised by a narcissistic mother, your attachment style is going to be insecure because the narcissistic mother does not know how to bond with her baby, feel empathy, or put the needs of her baby first. Her selfish mindset will lead her to feeling some resentment toward her child. This resentment stems from seeing the baby as someone infringing on her time, which interferes with her own needs. A narcissistic mother will often respond to her baby crying only when it suits her. This creates fear, stress, and lack of trust in the growing infant who does not have a way to manage her distress. The cycle continues to get worse as the baby cries and cries and her mother does not show the appropriate amount of empathy and love. As the baby withdraws and becomes more anxious, the narcissistic mother will also withdraw further because she will take the child's behavior personally. Attachment styles stemming from childhood can play a major role in how we function day-to-day.

Secure Attachment

This attachment style develops through trust. When an infant cries in distress, her caregiver responds with affection and attention. This secure attachment the baby experiences helps her trust and bond with others throughout her life. A strong foundation lets her develop loving and secure relationships more easily. She will be more likely to mature with healthy self-esteem, and thus she'll be more likely to avoid relationships that harm her mentally, emotionally, or physically. Raising a securely attached child takes dedication from parents. Parents must put a lot of focus on their child to learn their style of communication and their personality. A parent's attunement to a daughter allows the parent to anticipate her needs and respond quickly to them, building trust and a strong bond.

When a parent fails to provide the attention and care required to become deeply attuned to their child, that creates an insecure attachment. Intermittent response to the child's needs is especially difficult, as this creates anxiety in the child. She is unable to regulate her own emotions because she can't rely on a routine way of communicating with her caregiver that gets her the attention she needs.

Ambivalent Attachment

With ambivalent attachment, the child has learned that her mother will only attend to her needs occasionally. Daughters of narcissistic mothers learn early on that sometimes their mothers respond to them with resentment. As you can imagine, this is very confusing for a young child or an infant who is wired from birth to attach to her caregiver. Part of healthy attachment is aimed at ensuring that she is nurtured with essentials like food, water, and safety, but a child also needs emotional connection and love. This does not happen with a narcissistic mother.

When a narcissistic mother meets her child's physical needs but cannot connect with her emotionally, the child learns that she is a burden. A daughter in this situation may act out in a variety of ways to gain a form of emotional connection. As she grows older, she will not understand what it is to have a trusting and loving relationship and may be attracted to others who seem emotionally unavailable because this feeling is familiar to her.

With an ingrained sense of feeling unwanted, the adult daughter may sabotage relationships. Even with a romantic partner who is caring, her experience with an uncaring mother will lead her to be clingy or needy with her partner, to doubt their intentions, and to be hypervigilant for signs that they may walk away. Her insecurity, if left unchecked, will likely lead to self-fulfilling prophecy: these demands are overwhelming to a healthy partner, and the pattern of behavior she has learned may push them away. She will engage in unhealthy relationships repeatedly until she learns a healthier attachment style—and her own worth.

Avoidant Attachment

This attachment style, like the other insecure attachment styles, comes from inappropriate responses from the parent as the infant cries out to have her needs met. In avoidant attachment, when the mother does respond to her daughter's tears or distress, she is dismissive. She tells her daughter to stop crying, or to toughen up; in the case of an infant, she may give the baby a bottle and prop it up rather than take the time to bond during feeding. That's not to say that if you as a mother have done this you've disrupted your child's attachment. It only becomes a dysfunctional attachment style when this is the technique that the parent consistently uses.

When a parent repeatedly leaves the child on her own rather than actively soothing the child and bonding with her, the child learns to self-soothe because she knows she cannot rely on her caretaker to comfort her. The child then becomes more independent and adult-like. She learns not to express her emotions, and she shuts down her desire for connection, love, bonding, and comfort from others. The child becomes lonely, and she probably has a sense of emptiness. She may believe deep down that she is unworthy of love and respect. As an adult, she will not allow herself to feel close in romantic relationships, and she will likely feel uncomfortable as her relationships become more serious. She will be put off when her partner expresses their emotional needs. She may even avoid relationships altogether because she fears rejection.

Disoriented Attachment

This style is also known as "disorganized attachment" and occurs when the mother doesn't know how to react to her daughter's distress. The mother cannot provide a sense of safety to her child and, to a certain extent, she mirrors her child's emotions. When the infant daughter is fearful, the insecure mother may react fearfully rather than assuring her daughter that she is safe. The mother is anxious, and so her daughter cannot see her as someone who provides a sense of security.

The daughter tends to sense this helplessness in her mother and does not know what to make of it. She will internalize her mother's fears and anxieties. The daughter will come to see the world as a scary place with little to no refuge. As she grows up, she will be confused: a sense of insecurity has been instilled in her, and she will have a hard time understanding well-intentioned people around her. She will reverse roles with her mother, who will appear to be incapable of functioning due to her own fears. Thus, the daughter takes on the role of the protective parent and comforts or reassures her mother that she is safe. For a narcissistic mother, this feeds into her own self-importance. The mother thrives under her daughter's protection because it feeds her ego.

Attachment Injury

Attachment injury is a trauma in a relationship that disrupts or destroys bonding. This can be a betrayal, a lack of providing support and safety, or indifference to the needs of the other in the relationship.

As explored in the attachment styles above, these injuries can happen from birth and can significantly impact the daughter's relationships for the rest of her life. Unfortunately, with these insecure attachment styles, we often replay these roles in our romantic relationships as adults. You've likely heard that we tend to partner with someone similar to our parents. This occurs because there may be an unconscious desire to repair what was broken in the previous relationship through the new one. In a narcissistic mother-daughter relationship, the daughter will likely partner with someone who is similar to her mother. Because the daughter has suffered such a severe disruption in bonding, when she partners with someone in adulthood, she may view small fights or challenges as unforgiveable and the relationship might be forever changed. The daughter will view her partner as forever untrustworthy and start distancing herself from the relationship, further deepening her feeling of insecurity.

Supply, or narcissistic supply, is a term commonly used to describe the admiration, approval, affirmation, and attention the narcissist relies on to keep them going. To a narcissist, supply is somewhat like a drug, and without their supply, they go into withdrawal. They can get supply through awards or other types of recognition, but they cannot get it from within. Their supply is always external, and it is ultimately what defines them.

Social media is a haven for a narcissist to receive the supply for which she is so desperate. She will post a flattering photo of herself to receive compliments whenever she needs a "hit." Even negative attention can fuel her: she is not terribly picky about how she gains attention as long as she gets it. She can always manipulate the negative comments to her favor. For example, she can say people didn't like her picture because they're jealous of her, or she can play the victim when she receives negative attention. The supply is of utmost importance and is the reason she may have many people in her life who appear to be her friends or supporters. The ego of the narcissist is based on supply, and without it, she does not exist, so she works to maintain these relationships.

The Enabler

In the world of narcissism, the enabler is often a spouse or partner of the narcissist. Those in recovery from narcissistic abuse refer to the enabler as a "flying monkey." As you may know, flying monkeys were the creatures that protected and carried out the commands of the Wicked Witch of the West in *The Wizard of Oz*. The enabler maintains a long-term relationship with the narcissist and fills a role that keeps the narcissist content. The enabler can also be a friend who is codependent or easily manipulated. These are typically the only types of friendships narcissists have, since people who are not codependent or easily manipulated will not want to maintain a relationship with a narcissist long enough to fulfill this role.

The enabler will often defend the behaviors of the narcissist even though they may also be an ongoing victim of the narcissist's attacks. Submission to the narcissist keeps the enabler in a protected status. This special status means the narcissist will usually focus her rage and negativity on others. Enablers are rewarded for their loyalty with the praise and affection they crave from their narcissist. They have a sense of perceived status with the narcissist, in part because they tend to believe in her grandiose persona.

The enabler gains privilege and prestige by protecting the narcissist. The enabler will sacrifice their own children if they need to by blaming the children for some perceived wrong rather than standing up for the children and facing the rage of the narcissist. For the enabler, this can give them the sense of being in the good graces of the narcissist. The enabler is convinced they are protecting the children, or protecting others who are on the receiving end of the narcissist's bad behavior, insults, and rage. Unfortunately for the children of narcissists, this often means the parents are consumed by this cycle in their own relationship, leaving the children isolated, ignored, and often scapegoated.

Identifying the Enabler

The enabler has a stake in keeping the narcissist content. They have more peace and less emotional exhaustion when the narcissist feels adored, respected, and superior to others. The enabler can also have a good deal of empathy for the narcissist because they have likely seen her in vulnerable moments when the narcissistic mask has slipped.

To identify the enabler, be aware of their low tolerance for stress. Their emotional and mental energy is consumed by attending to the narcissist, and thus when the enabler is a parent, they are left with little patience or compassion for the needs of their children. As the daughter of an enabler, you may see a lack of empathy for you at the same time that your enabling parent is showing love and empathy for the narcissist. The children of narcissists are often shunted to the side. The enabler expects children to show respect to the narcissist despite the lack of respect the children receive from both the narcissist and the enabler. The enabler will invalidate the child's reactions to the narcissist's abuse to make sure the narcissist is kept happy. The enabler puts the narcissist's comfort first, even if that comfort comes at the cost of the child's happiness and security.

The following is a list of phrases that enablers commonly use to protect their narcissist by deflecting responsibility from her when she does something harmful. Generally, the enabler shifts the focus from the mother's actions to the child's "sensitivity." If you've noticed someone in your life saying at least four of these things, you can probably identify that person as an enabler.

→ "She didn't really mean it."
→ "Don't take things so personally."
→ "You're being too sensitive."
→ "Toughen up!"
→ "You know she can be this way."
→ "Try not to upset her."
→ "You made your mother cry. Go apologize."

Effects on Daughters

We've explored how important, and unique, the mother-daughter bond is. A damaged bond can be destructive to any child, but having no bond or an unstable bond is brutal to the daughter of a narcissistic mother. A daughter is valued for what she can achieve and how the achievements reflect on her mother. There is no unconditional love from her mother. The daughter of a narcissist always has to earn the mother's love, and that love is fleeting. To please her mother and to soothe herself, the daughter will adapt peculiar behaviors that function as survival mechanisms for her. She may dutifully clean the house from floor to ceiling before her mother returns from work to ensure a positive acknowledgement from her mother. She may turn to substances in an attempt to ignore the emotional void and loneliness she feels within herself. She is likely to involve herself in short-lived relationships in a desperate attempt to feel loved.

Lack of Self-Care

Many daughters of narcissistic mothers struggle profoundly with self-care. They may have a hard time accomplishing basic things that most of us do to care for ourselves, such as showering regularly, eating nutritious foods, staying hydrated, and getting regular sleep. Since most daughters of narcissistic mothers will likely show symptoms of depression, it's not surprising that these basic needs will go unmet, as many people with depression also have trouble with the caretaking tasks described above.

The daughter is not likely to find ways to help herself in this area unless she has a strong support system. She has to be encouraged to go against her learned behavior of putting others—particularly her mother—first. The daughter will claim that she is fine and will feel tremendous shame if she does anything for herself. She may finally decide to go to an exercise class but feel guilty the whole time she is there, thinking she should be doing something more valuable with her time. She feels like she must earn anything pleasant. She has not learned to love herself.

Self-Blame

As the daughter of a narcissist, do you often find yourself saying "I'm sorry" to the point that other people point it out to you? Clinicians see this frequently when adult daughters of narcissists finally learn to ask for help and seek therapy. In therapy, these women apologize for everything from coughing to asking when their next appointment will be.

What these women have learned from early on is that they will be blamed whether they have done something wrong or not. To avoid the exhaustion of trying to defend themselves, they have gotten into the habit of just apologizing to end the conflict.

The more insidious part of this phenomenon is that they actually think many problems are their fault. The daughter of a narcissist will typically believe that if she had done something differently or if she had been a different person, then things would have been better. She believes that she caused her mother's rage, and she takes full responsibility for provoking her. She learns more and more to deny herself and focus on her mother to make sure this does not happen again. The daughter of a narcissist internalizes the lies and distortions of her mother and her enablers.

Insecure Attachments

As you saw when reading about attachment styles, early childhood experiences steer the direction the daughter's relationships take later on. While secure attachment with a parent usually means happy and satisfying relationships, insecure attachment can lead to troubled relationships filled with turmoil. This is true not only for romantic relationships but also for friendships and professional acquaintances.

The daughter of a narcissist has usually learned to take a submissive role in all of her relationships, waiting and wanting to be accepted. As she did with her mother growing up, the daughter will take opportunities to gain approval from others through achievement or going overboard. She may volunteer to take the undesirable shift at work so that her work "friend" can go to a concert on a Friday night even if she herself had tickets to go to that concert, too. She may offer to watch her neighbors's dog or even their children while they go on a two-week vacation. It is the learned behavior of the daughter to put everyone else first out of fear of losing the relationship. This often leads to a lot of resentment, which eventually leaves the daughter feeling conflicted: while she needs the social connection, she resents the familiar feeling of being devalued.

Complex Post-Traumatic Stress Disorder (CPTSD)

I think most of us are familiar with PTSD, a disorder that develops after a person witnesses or experiences a horrific event. The diagnostic criteria for PTSD are rigid and limiting, and most therapists (myself included) see complex PTSD, or CPTSD, in our practices more often than we see the more narrowly defined PTSD.

People with CPTSD can have some of the same symptoms of PTSD, including hypervigilance, intrusive thoughts or images, nightmares, and feeing emotionally numb and detached. There are additional symptoms in CPTSD that are not necessarily evident in PTSD, such as an inability to manage emotions, unstable relationships, dissociation, and a distorted view of the abusive person or people in her life. It's these symptoms that typically become unbearable and lead people to therapy.

Depression and anxiety are inherent to CPTSD and PTSD, and women are more likely to seek help for the symptoms related to these disorders. If there is an underlying trauma disorder, however, their depression and anxiety are only part of the problem. With some of the most severe narcissistic abuse, women have been on a plethora of different medications and found no relief. Medications cannot help increase a person's self-esteem, nor can they help one feel as though one has value after a lifetime of being told that their value is conditional.

Mistrust

The daughter of a narcissist has learned that she cannot count on others. As you recall, her needs were not met consistently as a child, which led to an overall mistrust of others. When she grows up, her mistrust becomes an inherent part of her relationships. She has likely gravitated toward people who seem familiar to her which, unfortunately, means people similar to her mother. Even if she is drawn to someone who reminds her of the enabler, she will not trust that person because she has seen the lengths her mother's enablers have gone to in keeping her happy. As a child, the daughter watched the enabler neglect her in favor of her mother's comfort.

This learned mistrust can be so damaging that the daughter will miss out on relationships and opportunities in her attempts to protect herself. Even when she gets involved in a healthy romantic relationship, she might sabotage it due to her inability to trust that another person can love her for who she is. She will convince herself that the relationship is not serious or worth nurturing and may walk away from it "before she gets hurt" because she believes she inevitably will. Though this book, you will learn that you can have loving and secure relationships, and you deserve them.

Self-Harming Tendencies

Narcissistic mothers do not model a healthy way to manage emotions, nor do they validate their daughters' feelings and help them work through pain. As adults, these daughters may use forms of self-harm to avoid experiencing their feelings. They have never learned to manage emotion and are overwhelmed by feelings of sadness or anger. These women cannot express their feelings without fear of losing complete control of themselves, and so they turn to self-harm as a coping mechanism.

Some women come into my practice with the telltale scars of cutting on their forearms and other exposed parts of their skin. My practice is in a state where recreational use of marijuana is legal, and since that law came into effect, women have spoken much more freely of their use of marijuana to manage their anxiety and to help them sleep at night. Clients report abusing alcohol and other substances because sitting with the feelings of worthlessness and inadequacy that have accumulated over the years is unbearable. Eating disorders or unhealthy, obsessive relationships with food are also common in these women because their mothers have emphasized the importance of an "ideal" appearance.

Self-Gaslighting

There is definitely a pattern to narcissistic abuse, and the daughter of a narcissist learns to torture herself with the same kinds of behaviors and actions that her abuser inflicted on her.

As part of her manipulation, a narcissistic mother repeatedly tells her daughter that her perceptions of reality are incorrect and that the way she feels or the opinions she has are invalid or unimportant. Daughters of narcissistic mothers internalize this gaslighting dialogue. We typically hear about being gaslit by others, but it's also extremely common for us to gaslight ourselves.

The narcissist convinces her daughter that her perception of reality is not accurate. This can become dangerous, because the daughter also learns to ignore her intuition. If the adult daughter of a narcissist hears alarm bells when her new boyfriend "lovingly" says she would look prettier with her hair longer, she convinces herself that there must be something wrong with her, not her boyfriend. She ignores her intuition and chalks it up to some deficiency of her own.

Shawna Embraces the Truth

Shawna came to me in the middle of her relationship with a man who made Shawna feel as if she was
going crazy. She was beside herself that she could
allow a man like Jason into her life, and she had done
some research on her own and discovered that he
had many narcissistic traits. I have never met Jason,
but from Shawna's description, I would agree. He
played all the classic narcissistic games with her,
and she fell for all of them despite being a successful, well-educated woman.

She does not understand for the life of her how
she got to where she is today. She has made several attempts to sever contact with him, and he, of
course, never respects her boundaries. She tried to
avoid him, but this became more difficult after he
bought a house only blocks away from her after she
broke up with him. She still holds an affinity for him,
and only after two years of therapy did she begin to
explore the roots of why she let someone like him
into her life.

When Shawna was finally ready to delve into her
vulnerabilities, she started to recognize how harshly
her mother had criticized her growing up. This led
to more conversation, and Shawna began to recognize that despite telling me early on how normal and
happy her childhood was, she rolled her eyes every
single time she mentioned her mother in therapy. As

we tiptoed into this area, Shawna slowly came to see that there was a reason her sister moved away the second she was old enough to leave the family home. She came to see that there was a reason her brother distanced himself from the family.

Shawna had her first realization when her mother was coming for a visit: she said she had to make sure she cleaned her house meticulously and hid any new items she bought since her mother's last visit because she didn't want to give her mother "an excuse" to belittle her. These are skills she has learned and keeps up as an adult, despite being financially independent and having children of her own. She goes to great lengths to remove any ammunition her mother might have to devalue Shawna.

She is loyal to her mother to a fault, and the dynamic between the two is harmful to Shawna. The patterns established in Shawna's relationship with her mother—the gaslighting and the criticism—all led to Shawna not trusting her intuition when she started seeing signs that Jason was abusive. She stayed in the relationship even though he was unfaithful and manipulative. She believed his preposterous stories about spending time with past girlfriends because he was "helping them through a tough time" or some other heroic, self-sacrificing reason he manufactured. Because she learned not to trust her own perceptions from an early age, Shawna fell for these stories completely.

CHAPTER TWO REVIEW

After reading this chapter, I hope you have found validation and maybe an inkling (or more) of love and respect for
yourself. You have managed to start working on yourself
even with so many obstacles set in your path from the
get-go. I hope you are beginning to see that you have survived insidious narcissistic abuse from your own mother.
You've likely blamed yourself for failed relationships and
maybe even wished you could go back and do things differently because you believed that the failure was all your
fault. I hope you have a deeper understanding of why you've
put so much blame and responsibility on yourself, and how
absolutely undeserving of this blame you are. Ideally, you
now have an idea of the importance of self-care, so you can
function to the best of your abilities.

Moving forward, keep in mind:
- → You are worthwhile and deserving, and the
  damage to your self-esteem can be undone.
- → Relationships from your past were not healthy
  because you had nothing modeled for you and
  no understanding of what a healthy, recipro-
  cal relationship looked or felt like. You did not
  know that it was not okay to be insulted, and
  maybe you didn't realize that your partner was
  gaslighting you.
- → You can learn to see that your mistrust, depression, anxiety, and need to self-medicate or
  self-harm are all the result of abuse.
- → You did not get the care you deserved as a child,
  and that will always be unfair. But as an adult,
  you can work to heal yourself, and you can learn
  to give yourself the care and love you need.

PART TWO

RECOVERING FROM THE NARCISSISTIC MOTHER

Now that you have a better idea of what narcissistic personality disorder is, how it develops, and more specifically how this disorder affects daughters of narcissistic mothers, we will explore approaches to recovery. There are many ways you can start to repair the significant damage a narcissist can cause. We will look at how to fully understand what you are feeling and also how to make sense of your experiences after a lifetime of being told your perception of reality is incorrect. You will learn to understand and trust your emotions and how your body reacts to abuse. You will be given tools to manage your relationship with your mother so that you feel more in control of how you are treated.

Ultimately, the goal is for you to build up your self-worth enough to expect respectful treatment from your mother and others. Sometimes the healthiest thing you can do is remove yourself from the relationship with your mother altogether; we will delve into how to sever ties with one's mother in a way that won't cause a spiral of guilt.

Through your hard work and introspection, you will learn to bolster your self-esteem and trust your intuition. You will learn to trust that you matter, and your thoughts and opinions matter as well. You will start to notice the other toxic relationships in your life. As you come into your own power, toxic relationships will become intolerable to you because you will know that you deserve better. You will learn to love, care for, and validate yourself.

CHAPTER THREE

Processing Your Emotions

You've probably heard of processing your emotions, but let's explore what that actually means. To process your emotions, you need to identify what they are in the first place. This is incredibly difficult for people who have spent their lives putting the emotions and needs of someone else first. You've likely seen your mother crying, raging, responding coldly, or even being sweet, but you have not noticed a consistent pattern to her behaviors. Since the understanding of emotions typically comes from the modeling of a caregiver, you have likely been very confused about your own feelings at times.

You have to learn to identify your own feelings before you are able to process them, and processing is extremely important to your future. Without understanding and uncovering what you've been through and how your experiences made you feel, you cannot have a clear understanding or a connection with others. You will likely find yourself in a state of fight, flight, freeze, or fawn when in the face of difficult situations. Those impulses may cause you to stay stuck in a survival pattern rather than a pattern of living exuberantly. You aren't doomed to follow those impulses forever, though: you can change, and you can live a better, fuller life.

The Power of Feeling

The path to identifying and understanding your emotions is a worthwhile one. It will lead to you discovering who you really are and what is important to you. When you learn what your emotions are, you will also learn why a feeling in your stomach is present and to trust it. You will start to notice your intuition—your gut reaction—and you will learn to trust that, too. Your intuition can be your guardian angel. It will protect you from people who do not deserve your time and energy, and it will lead you to those who do. Our emotions help us understand what we want and, more important, what we don't want. Tuning in to our feelings and desires helps build our identities. Emotions help us understand situations that we find ourselves in. They also help us understand who we are and how to navigate relationships and conflict in a healthier fashion.

Naming

The first step in processing your emotions is knowing what they are. When you've spent most of your emotional energy on someone else, you forgo developing a strong sense or understanding of your own emotions. When feelings arise that you cannot label, you can't move forward with processing them. When that happens, you don't understand or cannot tolerate the way you are feeling, and as a result, you will likely do everything in your power to make the feeling go away. This is one way that addictions and unhealthy behaviors manifest. We might see abuse of substances, eating disorders, or process addictions such as shopping because the emotions are so uncomfortable that we cannot sit with them.

Anger is an emotion that most of us can recognize, but what you may not know is that most therapists see anger as a secondary emotion. It's secondary because it has roots in other emotions: anger protects us from feeling vulnerable and it is likely distracting us from recognizing what is really going on with us. Anger can cover up feelings of rejection, embarrassment, hurt, fear, frustration, indignation—the list goes on. There are seven basic emotions: joy, surprise, sadness, disgust, anger, fear, and happiness. I have included fear in this list because it is so easily recognizable and relatable, but like anger, it often covers up more vulnerable emotions. You need to know what your emotions are and what they feel like in your body. Really tune in to your emotions. Take the time to think about what caused them.

Mindfulness

Notice that I have used both the word "emotion" and the word "feeling." We absolutely feel our emotions in our bodies. An important tool in recognizing, understanding, and processing emotion is mindfulness. This is a trendy concept for good reason. Practicing mindfulness will help you be more aware of what is happening in the moment, both within yourself and outside yourself. It's easy to go through life on autopilot, and so it takes a lot of practice to change the way you are used to thinking about the world around you. Being mindful takes a great deal of concentration and self-compassion because there will be many times that your mind will drift to something other than what you are doing or experiencing in the moment. When your mind wanders, you will have to bring your attention back to the present. Mindfulness is paying attention to only what is

happening in the moment. This attention helps you understand your reactions and responses to the interactions you
have with others. It is fairly easy to start being mindful on
your own, no matter the time or location. Mindfulness is
about awareness without judgment.

Notice the details of the paint strokes on the walls of the
room you're in, pay attention to the beauty of the flowers
you see when you take a walk, listen to the sounds of birds
outside, notice the smells of the food you're cooking, pay
attention to the way the fur feels when you're snuggling
with your pet. All of these daily activities are perfect ways
to start your mindfulness practice. Be deeply aware of the
present moment you're in. This is especially valuable for
the daughters of narcissistic mothers, who are so often
trapped in the past. You may carry around a sense of regret
over what could have been, but mindfulness can help bring
you back into the present.

Acceptance

You might recognize that you have been living with two
different realities of your own history. Through one lens,
you had a happy childhood during which your mother
always dressed you well and pushed you to excel in school
or other activities. When you look through another lens,
you recognize that you were under a lot of pressure to look
good and to perform well to meet your mother's expectations. As an adult, it is difficult to understand what you felt
as a child and which of the two lenses actually shows your
reality. Working this out is perhaps the most important
step of all. It may feel strange or unnecessary, but it is the
most liberating thing you can do for yourself.

The human mind wants balance and a logical understanding of the world around us. We expect justice and
fairness, and we have a very difficult time accepting any
disparity. The truth is that many events are not fair. Healing

from your relationship with your narcissistic mother is never going to feel right until you accept the truth of your relationship. I have heard clients state that they want their mothers to understand the pain they have caused, take responsibility for being inadequate parents, and apologize for the destruction they caused in their lives. These things are very unlikely to happen; if they do, they won't feel genuine and you will almost certainly see no lasting change in your mother's behavior. This may be the saddest and most difficult part of your journey, but I promise you, once you have accepted things for the way they are, you will truly be free.

Sandra's Journey Toward Acceptance

Sandra came to therapy to help manage her relationship with her mother, who was quite involved with Sandra's daily life. Her mother had recently come to live with her for a while, as Sandra had just given birth for the first time—to twins. While Sandra really needed her mother's help with the babies, she soon found herself wanting to get as far away from her mother as she could. Sandra came to my office and said, "I feel like I'm going crazy." Every one of my narcissistic abuse survivor clients says they feel crazy, no matter who their abuser is.

Until she had her own little girls, Sandra never understood that her mother's behavior was abnormal, much less abusive. Sandra felt a love for her daughters that she had never experienced before, and she thought her mother must have had a similar experience when she gave birth to Sandra. Then, a feeling in the pit of her stomach told her something different.

As we worked together, Sandra recognized that her mother's interest in the girls was more about an image than wanting to spend quality time with Sandra or the girls. The attention her mother received from the girls fed Sandra's mother's ego but drained Sandra. The dynamic took her back in time to when she was her mother's trophy child. When Sandra started to understand her mother's behavior and label her mother's narcissistic traits, she was able to start the work of recovery and recognize her own self-worth. In therapy, Sandra and I spent a great deal of time going over her own understanding of the seven different emotions, and she began to trust her reactions. She started practicing mindfulness and increased her participation in yoga. She began to focus on where tension lived within her body.

The most difficult part of the journey for Sandra was accepting that her childhood was not the healthy version she lied to herself about. Instead, it was emotionally abusive, and she was neglected as her mother pursued her own activities to receive her narcissistic supply. Coming to this truth broke Sandra's heart. She longed for attention and affection from her mother and never understood why she did not receive it. When she began to accept that she did not get what every child deserves, she also recognized that it was not because she was not good enough. She saw that she was raised by someone who was profoundly damaged and incapable of providing the love and affection a child needs. She grieved the loss of what never was and eventually accepted the reality. She knows now that she has the capacity to love and nurture her inner child and her own children.

When Home Doesn't Feel Safe

The person you were supposed to be able to rely on the most was not a protector for you. She did not have the capacity to let you know that you were loved and that you mattered. You were never securely attached to her, and as you got older, it only got worse. In many ways, you were on your own. You had to figure out how to fly under the radar and what kind of recognition she wanted from you day-to-day. You didn't have an ally. Perhaps you had another parent in the house who was also trying to stay under the radar and not be the target for abuse. If you had siblings, they, too, were trying to navigate the ever-changing expectations of your mother.

Being raised in this environment is confusing and encourages a family culture of every-person-for-themselves. No child can feel secure being raised in an environment like this. Every day is filled with instability. When you were a child growing up with a narcissistic mother, you lacked structure and routine. In this chaotic setting, you didn't feel safe. You were constantly in emotional survival mode with no room to let your guard down or even have fun. As you developed through life and started having relationships outside of the home, you didn't intrinsically know who was trustworthy and who was not.

Our adult relationships are profoundly influenced by our pasts. We are often drawn to what is familiar and, unfortunately, if narcissists are familiar, we can feel drawn to narcissists or otherwise emotionally abusive people. Many daughters of narcissistic mothers end up in romantic relationships that are abusive.

Furthermore, you know that there is no safe home to return to, because it never existed for you. There is likely no one to turn to from your family of origin if they are still wrapped up in the dysfunction. You have no safe support system because you have been too cautious with others to develop a strong support network. Things can seem incredibly hopeless, and having no safe home to return to can keep a person in a constant cycle of abuse. You need to commit to the steps you will take toward your own recovery to put an end to this cycle. Be patient and gentle with yourself. You've got this!

Dissecting Vulnerability and Shame

Some forms of shame do serve a valuable purpose. Shame can teach us what is acceptable and what is not acceptable.

But the shame stoked by a narcissist only trains you to hate yourself. If you're out in public and your mother tells you your hair would be so much cuter if it were styled differently, what are you going to focus on? You will notice how everyone else has styled their hair, and you will harshly criticize your own. The voice of shame goes from being your mother's to your own, leaving you feeling vulnerable with every interaction. You may even start over-apologizing since you have been programmed to believe all bad things are your fault.

This shame has now become your internal voice, and the voice does not say kind things to you. It convinces you that you have no worth, and so you spend your time trying to prove that you are worthy. You may be highly educated and have a prestigious job, but somehow you are still unfulfilled. You have felt too vulnerable to allow yourself to explore your feelings, and you stay extremely active to show that you matter. Daughters of narcissistic mothers often look as though they have it all figured out, but in reality, there is a huge void that you are trying to hide from the world. This void will never go away on its own, and even when you've accomplished all your goals, you may still feel empty. In a really unhealthy and destructive way, you may also feel guilty for feeling dissatisfied. You've got everything you've always wanted and you're still unhappy. Nearly every narcissistic abuse survivor I work with feels this way, so you are not alone. Your feelings are valid. Processing your emotions and understanding the path that made you who you are will remove you from this vicious cycle of guilt and shame.

Guilt Management

The mother-daughter relationship is put on a pedestal. It can be hard to imagine that a daughter could have a good reason to separate herself from her mother. Even people who know firsthand how toxic a mother can be may buy into the myth of the mother-saint, because there are so many messages around us saying that we must honor and respect our parents no matter what.

You may feel guilty because you can't muster up the energy to buy a Mother's Day card that you don't want to send (your body is telling you something there). When you realize how much you are controlled by shame, you can start to put boundaries in place in order to avoid falling victim to unreasonable expectations. Establishing strong boundaries is a way to protect yourself. Strong boundaries can also interrupt unhealthy patterns in relationships.

Please be aware that when you start placing and enforcing boundaries, you are going to feel guilty. People around you, especially your mother, will challenge your boundaries and use shame and guilt to manipulate you into going back to the status quo. Don't fall for it. You can even use these interactions as validation that you are on the right track of your recovery process. Your determination will pay off. Letting go of guilt and maintaining boundaries will change your life and help you figure out who you are and what matters to you the most. This is how you will rebuild your identity. You will learn that it is okay to stand up for what is right for you and expect kindness, consideration, and respect from others. You do not have to tolerate abusive behavior from your mother. Most of all, setting up your boundaries and learning to maintain them will validate for you that it is okay to say no to anything that does not feel right to you.

When my clients get to this part of their process, I often hear that they feel like they are exhibiting narcissistic traits by becoming focused on what is right for them. Some clients will put up more boundaries than necessary and then settle toward a middle ground. Even though you may feel that you are being somewhat narcissistic in creating your boundaries, please remember that this should have been part of your natural development. You should have been allowed to set boundaries starting in childhood, but that experience was taken from you. This is your time to go back and nurture that inner child and allow her the right to be a little self-centered in figuring out what is best for her. Change is incredibly difficult, and it takes a lot of work. But if you do the work, you will start to see that you are worthy of your own care, and you are worthy of respectful treatment from others.

Getting Rid of Guilt

Not all guilt is bad. When we've done something against our own standards, our guilt can motivate us to correct it. In those cases, guilt helps us move forward. Irrational guilt is when we take responsibility for things we did not have any part in. Simply by existing, we feel as though we've done something wrong. This irrational guilt will never cease until we correct the irrational thoughts that feed into this guilt. Dialectical behavioral therapy has amazing tools for managing emotions, specifically guilt. In her book *DBT Skills Training Handouts and Worksheets*, Marsha M. Linehan lays out some strategies:

→ First, do a reality check. You're feeling guilty, but what led to this feeling? What are the facts? Does your guilt align with the facts? If not, this would be a good time to look at where the disconnect is and correct your thinking.

→ Another approach is to act in a way that is the opposite of what you're feeling. If you're feeling guilty and can't figure out why, force yourself to be confident in your decision or action. If you make a habit of this, your feelings will better align with your actions. Eventually, your first response won't be to take the blame.

→ Finally, resolve the problem if there actually is one. If something did happen that you do feel responsible for, own up to it, apologize, and make it right. When guilty feelings are legitimate, take responsibility. This is a surefire way to make certain the guilt doesn't stay with you.

CHAPTER THREE REVIEW

Simply by being the daughter of a narcissistic mother, you are a survivor of emotional abuse and neglect. Suffering through years and years of abuse takes time and effort to heal, but there is hope. Always keep your eyes on the goal of recovery.

In this chapter, you have learned the following:

→ Emotions are powerful, and they have been used to control and manipulate you.

→ Emotions do not define you, and they come and go like waves. You can learn to ride them instead of being drowned by them.

→ Your feelings of insecurity and unworthiness are not real. Your mother told you a story about yourself to keep you in line.

→ You can create your own safety and you can learn to love who you are.

→ Shame comes from outside of you, and you can choose to reject it. Inappropriate feelings of shame no longer need to be part of your reality. You can process your guilt and move on from it.

→ Ultimately, you have so much more control over how you move forward than you may have realized.

CHAPTER FOUR

Managing Your Relationship

In this chapter, we will explore how to manage your relationship with your mother. You will set the terms of your relationship. Up to this point, the relationship you have had with her has likely been volatile and one-sided. You will learn more about establishing boundaries and the importance of maintaining them for your own peace of mind.

You will also learn strategies to manage the times when you miss your mother and uncover why you experience this feeling even though you now recognize her behavior as abusive. We will take a look at your triggers, where they come from, how they interfere with recovery, and even how they influence your other relationships. We will discuss removing yourself from your relationship with your mother altogether or temporarily, whichever is best for you. The power is now in your hands.

Deactivate Your Triggers

When you learned to identify your emotions, you also learned to recognize how and why you feel a certain way. The next step is to recognize variables in your environment—triggers—that can make those emotions come up. Although we may not be aware of why we feel something the very moment we feel it, emotions almost always have root causes.

You can be triggered by something as obvious as driving by your childhood home or something as subtle as seeing a person in a commercial who reminds you of a harmful experience. In the first example, certainly you can avoid this trigger by avoiding your childhood home. But for triggers that you are not able to avoid, you will have to dig deeper to find a solution. Below are some practices that you can incorporate with the other skills you've learned thus far.

Identify Triggers

An emotional trigger is an experience that takes us back in time and generates the same emotional reaction we felt when the initial negative event occurred. We might respond with the same intense rage or fear we responded with initially.

This emotional response may be expected. For example, when you watch a movie where a family loses a pet, thoughts of your own deceased pet may resurface the intense sadness you felt. Other emotional reactions may take you by surprise. You could be bewildered as to why you flew into a rage when someone cut you off while driving. There does not need to be a direct correlation between the current event and the experience that it reminds you of, but your emotional reaction could be the same. Someone cutting you off may cause you to feel rage, but if you look deeper, it could be fear that feels like the unpredictable or unsafe environment in which you grew up.

Mindfulness is essential in learning to recognize these reactions. Sit with your reaction and take time to identify the feeling. When you trace it back to a time you may have felt the same way in the past, you will start to uncover your triggers. Understanding your triggers is a giant step toward helping identify your emotions and why you are feeling them. It will also allow you to understand, validate, and manage your reactions.

Track Origin

Let's drill down a little more into where these emotions originated. We know that you likely did not have a lot of time to understand how you were feeling when you were growing up. Your attention was elsewhere. You were trying to figure out how to stay in the good graces of your mother; maybe you were strategizing to avoid being the target of her rage. When you are in survival mode, there is no room for emotional growth. When you did feel an emotion, you were likely told that you were wrong for feeling how you did. Your mother might have even said that you didn't truly feel what you said you felt. You did not have the time, nurturing, or validation to understand your emotions.

Thankfully, it's not too late to learn about the many different types of emotions we feel as human beings and try to put labels on what your body is telling you when you are triggered. Certainly, if someone cuts you off on the freeway, you might react with anger and colorful language. But digging a little deeper, does it feel like you don't have control? Does the other driver's behavior feel wildly unpredictable and scary? Identifying what it feels like and allowing yourself some time to connect this feeling back to when you felt this way before will give you a better understanding of your reactions.

Be Aware

You are likely experiencing emotional reactions far more frequently than you realize. You may notice that part of your body is aching for no apparent reason or that you have tension in your throat, back, shoulders, or chest. You may have stomach aches that seem to have no cause. When you have a headache that starts right when you walk in to work and ends on your drive home, it's worth figuring out what is happening. When you've ruled out environmental causes for this headache, it's time to start looking at how you feel about your job. The same can be said about any environment or relationship that gives you a knot in your stomach, tension in your throat, or any other physical reaction.

Being aware of what your body is telling you and understanding your triggers can help you identify your emotions and gain control over how you manage your environment. When you have this understanding, you can better determine whether your reactions fit the situation. In some cases, you will see that your reaction is not appropriate to the situation, and it is rooted in pain from your past.

Reprogram

Now you get to start understanding your own emotions and how you manage them. You get to remind yourself that the person who cut you off on the freeway is more likely late for work than personally trying to anger or scare you. You now have an understanding of where the fear came from instead of spending time dwelling on the reason this stranger in another car was so rude. You get to acknowledge that although your fear was real, it was not necessarily the most appropriate reaction to what was happening. You have some control in the situation, and you can do things like leave more space between your car and the car in front of you.

Understanding your triggers and emotions gives you power over them, and you will no longer need to question whether you overreacted or behaved poorly because you can now connect the dots of current and past emotion. You now get to tell your inner child that she is safe and she is no longer neglected. You get to comfort yourself when you're afraid or tell yourself it's okay to feel angry when you've been wronged.

You also have the sublime gift of knowing that emotions are not who you are. As a child, when you reacted with emotions that you did not understand, you were invalidated. Maybe your mother told you that you were irrational or crazy. Those words likely became self-talk in your mind. You now have the knowledge and power to be kind to yourself and understand who you are and why you respond to certain events in certain ways.

Setting Boundaries

Now that you have a better understanding of how and what you are feeling, it's time to learn tools to maintain a level playing field when it comes to your relationship with your mother. This is going to be challenging because she is not used to you giving her limits. Your mother is used to being the one in control and the one who knows best. You've been a reliable supply to her ego as well as a scapegoat for her shortcomings. When you set limits, she is going to try to fight them with every bit of ammunition available to her. Setting boundaries, however, is essential if you plan to continue your relationship with your mother. Be aware that this is going to be one of the most difficult and transformative parts of your journey towards recovery.

Set Your Agenda

Before you set boundaries, you have to figure out what you are trying to protect within yourself. Understanding your values is the first step. Let's start with respect. If this is something you have identified as valuable to you, it's important to set up a boundary that allows you to keep respect for yourself and for your mother. This is because showing her disrespect will give her an excuse to show disrespect to you.

When you are creating a boundary, you will have to teach it to your mother. To do this, you will have to make her aware of your expectations, then call her out when she crosses a line and redirect her. If she tells you that you've put on weight and should go on a diet and this feels disrespectful to you, it's important to address this comment in the moment. You can say something like, "I appreciate your concern, but this is a topic I would prefer not to talk about with you." Keep repeating the line every time she tries to talk about your body. It will become easier to speak up to her as you become more confident in standing your ground.

She will challenge you and remind you that every time she has spoken to you about your weight in the past, you never seemed to have a problem with it. It's okay to tell her, respectfully, that discussion about your appearance has always made you uncomfortable and that you want it to stop. Do not engage any further on the topic that is off-limits to you. This is your limit, and you are entitled to it.

Avoid Justification or Oversharing

Setting boundaries with a narcissist, especially your own mother, is going to be a battle of wills in the beginning. Your mother will try to convince you that the boundaries are not necessary and that you two are just close. She might also tell you that as your mother, she should know everything about you and be able to say anything to you. You will likely feel a strong urge to justify the reason you need to have boundaries with her and voice what she has done to make you need them in the first place. Our brains always want balance and justice. It's going to be difficult to avoid justifying your decision, because if someone set a new boundary for you, then you would want to know why.

But it's important to remember that your mother does not think the same way you do. You have empathy and want her to understand where you're coming from, but she has very little empathy and will only see that she is losing control of you. You might also be tempted to overshare. The danger here is that you might want to bring up how hurt you are by her behavior and actions. Don't fall into this trap. She will use your vulnerability to convince you that you do not need your boundaries and she never meant to hurt you. Nothing will change unless you hold your ground. Your persistence will pay off.

Keep Perspective

You have had a lifetime of a certain style of interaction with your mother. Your relationship is a dance you two have practiced throughout your entire life: she had power and control, and you tried your best to keep her happy. It's so easy to revert to a more childlike version of yourself when you are around your parents, no matter how old you are. It's also easy and common to get lost in this relationship dynamic and lose focus on your goals. As a result, you must continually remind yourself that you are an adult and you are no longer under the authority of your mother. It may help to tell yourself that your thoughts and values matter. You must keep reminding yourself that you are no longer a little girl just trying to survive in a world run by your mother. Instead, you are now an independent adult who can play by her own rules.

You can accept yourself just as you are. This may not come naturally to you, and that's okay. You will have to work hard at keeping and maintaining your perspective. Allowing yourself to exist as you are when you are in your mother's presence will help you maintain your power and grow into a stronger version of yourself than you have ever known.

Create an Exit Plan

This is all going to take a lot of effort! You will need to step out of the routine of how you relate to your mother. It may be hard to fathom, but you need to make an exit plan if you're going to break out of your old patterns with her. You need an exit plan because you
have to be okay with giving your mother, and maybe your other parent if he or she is an enabler, consequences for violating your boundaries. Just as you will have to explain what your limits are, you will have to explain and then follow through with consequences for crossing your boundaries.

It is important to make it very clear that you will leave the conversation or interaction with your mother if you are feeling disrespected and/or your boundaries are being ignored. Allow yourself to remove yourself from the interaction. Even if you share the same home with your mother, you must leave the room. There is always a way to remove yourself from the situation: hang up the phone, leave the house, go for a long walk with your phone turned off, refuse to speak with her. If you can't physically get away from her, you can tell her you will no longer engage in the conversation.

You can't control what other people do, but you can control what kind of behavior you accept from another person. You are not obligated to accept abusive behavior.

Open Communication

Many of us find ourselves exhausted after spending time with our narcissist. We often feel like our brain is in a fog even when the interaction was seemingly innocuous. The reason you might feel this way is because the emotional and mental games never stop, nor does the manipulation. Now that you have a better idea of how important boundaries are, it's time to look at how open communication will support your boundaries. As you create this new way of relating to your mother, it will be important to keep communicating to her what you're doing and why you're doing it. She needs to see that you are consistent and unwavering in your determination to change the dynamic you two have shared for so long.

Accuracy

As you are in the process of maintaining the boundaries you have set, it is important to be clear in what you say so that you reduce the risk of your words being twisted. Be concise with your words and clarify your mother's words, even though it may feel strange and rigid. This is necessary as you shift toward interacting with her in a way that empowers you.

Before you go to the length of making your exit to get your point across, it is necessary to make sure you have a clear understanding of how you got here. You will be on unstable emotional ground as you and your mother learn this new way of communicating, so you will want to make sure you are clear about what you said to her and what she said to you. Using our previous example, if your mother says something about your weight after you've set your boundary around that topic, you will want to verify with her that she suggested you go on a diet. Then explain to her that this crosses your boundary and enact your exit plan.

Direct Requests

Be concise with your requests so there is no misunderstanding of what you need or expect. If you ask your mother to watch your children, make sure that you have asked for exactly what you need and you have communicated any limitations around the request. If she overstays her welcome or does activities with your children that are not okay with you, make that clear. Do not let your need for a babysitter allow your boundaries to waver. In the moment, you may see your need as desperate, and she may try to use that to her advantage. Remember that there are other options. We can easily let our guard down when we are feeling pressure, so in these situations it is important to keep perspective. If your mother makes requests of you, the same rules apply. Be sure to be clear about what you are willing to do for her and what you are not.

Remaining Calm

Throughout this whole new endeavor, you are going to have times when your emotions are elevated (to say the least). This is to be expected, and hopefully you are learning to understand your feelings. As you're forging ahead with this new version of a relationship, try not to let your mother see any loss of emotional control that you may be feeling. You can cry and scream when your interaction with her is over, but if she sees it, she will twist your words around to invalidate what you're saying. That will be a direct trip back to your history with her.

Think of your calm demeanor as your shield: it will protect you and keep you on track in your interactions with your mother. If she sees you getting heated or upset, it will be as if she has found cracks in your shield that she can push through. I am always a proponent of feeling your emotions and expressing them—except in this situation. Your emotional vulnerability will be an elixir for your mother to regain the power she so desperately wants back. Eventually, you will have more freedom to express your emotions, but only when it feels safe for you and your boundaries feel solid.

Separating from Your Mother

Some relationships with a narcissistic mother are beyond repair. This is incredibly tough, and choosing to separate from your mother is going to be one of the hardest decisions of your life. Unfortunately, this sometimes needs to happen in order for a daughter of a narcissistic mother to be able to heal. Severing ties might be terrifying to contemplate, or it might be a relief. Either way, it is a decision worth a lot of consideration so that you trust your choices and you stay on track to heal. When you've made this decision with confidence, you can ideally move forward without guilt or regret and fully embrace the new self-respecting version of yourself. You can focus on discovering who you are without remaining in the abusive relationship.

A Letter

In my opinion, the best way to communicate your intentions to separate from your mother is in writing. As we know, direct communication with her can be manipulative, confusing, circular, and degrading. You may never get your thoughts and desires across because your words will be twisted, and you might walk away from the conversation feeling confused and foggy. Narcissists do not like being rejected or discarded; they feel that privilege is only allowed to them. In a letter, you can express what you feel is happening in your relationship, the effect it has had on you, and why you feel you need to take this step. If you want to use this letter to end communication with her, it will be important to use language that does not invite conversation.

→ Use definitive language that lets your mother know that you will not be communicating with her moving forward.
→ Specifically ask her to respect your choice. Ask her not to reach out to you to discuss the letter or your decision.
→ Give context as to what led you to get to this point. Even though you have told her verbally a thousand times in your life, tell her again why you are making this choice.
→ Finally, tell her if the separation is permanent or if you would like to leave the possibility of a future relationship open, but only on your terms.

In Person

This option is a little riskier. If you choose this option, I would recommend that you take a supportive person with you to help you stay on track. This person will also be there for you when the conversation with your mother ends, which will be helpful to you because you'll need someone to remind you that you did what is best for you. As you might expect, a face-to-face conversation with your narcissistic mother is going to be tumultuous.

→ She will likely try to convince you the problem is all in your head or that you're too sensitive.
→ She will invalidate and minimize your intentions.
→ She will likely play the victim and attack you with harsh words.

This might be the ugliest conversation you've had with her yet. If you choose to do this in person, please take the time to really consider how this is best for you and how you will keep the conversation on topic. Consider how you will express to her why you need to protect yourself through no contact. Plan to tell her that going forward, you will not answer her calls or communicate with her in any way. Do not allow yourself to get caught up in sidetrack conversations, and consider having your support person give you a code word if they feel the conversation needs to end or redirect.

A Letter to Your Mother

Writing this letter will take a great deal of thought on your part. You will want to get your point across respectfully and thoroughly, leaving no room for her to question your intentions. The following steps, which take their lead from dialectical behavioral therapy, will help you write this letter in a proven and effective manner.

→ First, describe your relationship as you see it. Rely heavily on facts, such as your mother telling you that you need to go on a diet when you asked her how a new dress looked on you.

→ Next, explain how specific interactions affected you, using "I" statements. For example, "I felt hurt and inadequate when you said I should go on a diet."

→ Your next step is to explain what you want to happen now. Assert yourself even though it might be uncomfortable. It is time to say, "I think it is in my own best interest to remove myself from this relationship."

→ Say something that reinforces the behavior you expect from her. You could say something like this: "I appreciate you respecting my boundaries by not calling, texting, or trying to communicate with me in any way."

As you write this letter, remain confident and focused on your goals. Be firm with your boundaries. At the end of the letter, include a short recap of what you said. Reinforce in the closing of the letter that you do not plan to communicate with her moving forward and that you expect the same treatment in return.

When You Are the Primary Caregiver

Being the primary caregiver for your narcissistic mother does not mean that you have to revert to your childhood relationship with her or put up with any abuse because of her condition. You should be treated with kindness and respect. Always remember that you can leave any interaction or conversation with her whenever you need to. It doesn't matter if you are in her house, at the grocery store helping her shop, or taking her to her doctor's appointment. You do not have to engage in a conversation with her. If you can't physically leave her in the moment, you can let her know that you will be remaining silent for the rest of your time with her and you would appreciate the same treatment in return. You may need to fight feelings of guilt if you are her caretaker.

The most important thing to remember here is that your feelings are valid. Our feelings change and as we grow and learn to respect ourselves, and we may see things in a new light. Allow this all to exist within you. Explore the feelings you have. Is your guilt justified, or is this your old habit of being responsible for everything that goes bad? Allow yourself time to delve into your feelings and act upon them as you see fit. If you still feel boundaries are needed and as little contact as possible is necessary, then go with that. Only you know what is best for you. Don't let anyone else decide whether your decision is good or bad, because only you know the complete story.

Grieving the Relationship

Many of us are aware of the five stages of grief, but do you know that they have meaning outside of losses related to death? People grieve the loss of many things without recognizing that they are grieving. Grief plays a significant role in any narcissistic relationship, but it is especially relevant and difficult when you are grieving the loss of what you should have had in a parent and accept that you will never have the parent you deserve. You grieve for the little girl inside you who was neglected. You grieve the fact that you never had a mother who showed you how to develop properly or understand yourself. You grieve for the little girl who often had to be the adult and was deprived of a real childhood of her own. Grief is one of the hardest things to overcome, but you cannot move forward without grieving.

Denial

One of the five steps in the grieving process is denial. It's easy to understand that those who are grieving a death do not want to accept that the person is gone. When it comes to waking up to our own reality, grief and denial are more complicated. The person you are grieving is still alive, but as you heal, you realize how much you missed out on in your development and how wounded that left you. While you were growing up, you may not have recognized how bad things were because your circumstances were the only life you knew. It is hard to accept the truth that your parent is inadequate. Instead, you need to believe the few good times with your mother were the norm, and the more frequent, ugly times were the exception. When you heal, you will no longer deny the truth. You may cycle through the stages of grief, but you will ultimately welcome acceptance.

Anger

As you might suspect, anger is part of this process. When you get to the grief phase of your recovery journey, you have accepted your reality and can feel really angry about the way you have been treated. This feeling is totally valid, because you were truly injured. You have had so many hurdles in your development that you had to overcome later in life, which left you in a game of catch-up with your development. When you look back, you see how much of your time was wasted trying to appease your abuser or trying to understand yourself. These are trials that children with loving and nurturing parents do not have to endure. You are likely very angry that someone cared so little for you that they would use you for attention and then throw you away when they were getting their supply from someone "better." You have a lot to be angry about, and it is important to allow yourself to go through this phase freely.

Bargaining

This concept is more complex and might be easier to understand using the example of losing a loved one to death, especially unexpected death. Picture a husband filled with regret because if he had come home earlier, he could have taken his wife to work, but instead she took the train that derailed and caused her death. This is a form of bargaining. When it comes to your relationship with your narcissistic mother, you might wish that your best friend's mother was your mother or say to yourself, "If I just got straight As in school my mother would have loved me." Bargaining is something many of us do in many different situations, but it is futile. The true foundation of our recovery is radical acceptance of the situation as it is, and bargaining is the opposite of acceptance. The grief cycle is not a smooth transition from one stage to another.

The bargaining stage can feel like a step backward from anger, but it is natural for us to go through these cycles to get to the other side: emotional and mental health.

Depression

As you can imagine, depression is naturally a significant part of grief. Depression might be a bit more complicated for daughters of narcissists because it is harder to differentiate its origin. Depression can be organic (dysfunction of neurons in the brain) or situational (stemming from our environment). For daughters of narcissistic mothers, it could easily be both. We would certainly feel sad when we start to recognize that we were neglected as children and likely verbally and emotionally abused. But as children, perhaps we had the sadness of feeling lonely and unloved on top of our organic depression. This is an example of how your environment can worsen a psychological condition. You can imagine why it was difficult to enjoy what would normally be considered joyous events when the cards are stacked against you to this degree.

Acceptance

This stage is where we truly begin to break free of our chains. When we get to the point where we can accept everything that we have experienced for what it was, we have reached the foundation from which we will build the healed versions of ourselves. Many daughters do not see acceptance as a place of freedom, and it scares them to think that this is a goal worth reaching. Imagining acceptance can feel like defeat. It can seem counterintuitive to just accept that your mother was unloving and neglectful, and childhood was indeed as awful as you recall. No matter how much you fight against acceptance, it does not change the truth. The more one fights against the truth, the longer they will remain stuck and will not move along in their journey toward a healthy and fulfilling life. You were raised in an environment that did not make sense and your brain is always looking for logic and justice. You have a lot to fight against to get through this stage. It may be hard to swallow, but once you get to acceptance and really acknowledge the truth, you come alive.

CHAPTER FOUR REVIEW

I hope you have come to see the control you have over your future.

→ You have learned how to recognize and manage your triggers. You have seen how they can haunt you and keep you stuck in an unhealthy emotional cycle.

→ You have learned the immeasurable importance of creating and maintaining boundaries. This gives you the structure you need to direct your path toward recovery.

→ You have seen how important communication is in setting and enforcing boundaries. Without effective communication, there is no point to boundaries, as they will not be adhered to or respected.

→ You have an example of how to express yourself if you decide that the relationship with your mother is no longer something you want to be a part of.

→ Finally, you have learned that grief works with you, not against you. The grief process allows for the fresh start you need to move forward.

I know some of what you've read in this chapter can feel overwhelming and a bit frightening. Your growth involves a lot of worthwhile change. But once you embrace it, you will never look back.

CHAPTER FIVE

Breaking the Cycle

This chapter will explore how to change the legacy of narcissistic abuse not only in your life, but also for your children and future relationships. Perhaps you have heard that trauma is generational. As you've gained more understanding of your own experience, you may recognize that this is true. The generational impact of narcissistic abuse is especially complicated because so many of us play supporting roles for the narcissist in our families of origin. We also tend to gravitate to people who seem familiar to us, which keeps us in the cycle.

As you build your future, you may notice that you have perpetuated these roles in your adult relationships and perhaps with your children. The clients that have come to me to make changes are chain-breakers. The have decided that they need to heal and break the cycles that they have lived in. As you have seen, this process takes a lot of work and a good deal of time. It can feel like too tall a mountain to climb, but every step you take to reach the top is worth the effort. You can climb slowly, one step at a time. Hang in there!

Overcoming Trauma

In my work with survivors of narcissistic abuse, I occasionally see clients bristle at the idea that they have been abused, much less that they have experienced trauma. Sometimes labeling your experience as traumatic is off-putting because you have learned to be tough. Saying you were harmed can feel like admitting weakness, which is an unsafe place. Other times, you may not have been able to accept the reality of your life. The term "abuse" is widely used and may not fit your own narrative, but the reality is, if you were raised by a narcissistic mother you were almost certainly neglected as a child. Neglect is a form of abuse. Some children of narcissistic mothers have been physically and emotionally abused as well. Abuse is traumatic, and when we experience trauma, it changes the way our brains work and process information.

I have seen a significant number of patients who have post-traumatic stress disorder or complex post-traumatic stress disorder as a result of growing up with a narcissistic parent. Do note that while PTSD is a disorder that can be officially diagnosed, CPTSD has not yet been recognized officially in diagnostic manuals.

Many survivors of narcissistic abuse I've worked with experience dissociation. Dissociation is a common coping response to trauma: People are commonly unable to remember a traumatic event, temporarily or permanently, even if they have residual feelings like fear or anger associated with the experience. In other cases, dissociation from trauma takes the form of feeling disconnected: people may remember a traumatic event in great detail, but feel emotionally detached from the memory, as if they saw it on TV. Because children have so little power and so little control over their lives, they may be more likely to use dissociation as a coping mechanism for trauma. People learn to dissociate to try to keep themselves safe, and when memories that are too painful to deal with are triggered, they may go back into that dissociative state. Often, this means that they tune out of their surroundings, and they may get lost in their own thoughts to the point that they can lose track of time.

Hypervigilance is also a symptom of PTSD and CPTSD. It's another coping mechanism: because people experienced a one-time or ongoing trauma, they are constantly on guard in case the danger returns.

Whether you have a disorder or just retain disruptive coping mechanisms you learned as a child, you probably struggle with trauma-rooted behaviors as an adult. It's important to acknowledge that these behaviors protected you as a child, but you don't need them anymore. With the help of a therapist, you can start working to unlearn these coping mechanisms and replace them with healthier behaviors that bring you back to the present. You may want to try some of the following:

→ **Learn more about trauma and PTSD.** This knowledge can help you understand what you're going through; it will also help you see that you're not alone.

→ **Join a local trauma support group.** Many people find this affirming, and researchers have found that people who have a social support network are more likely to recover from PTSD.

→ **Remind yourself that trauma responses are normal, and that the past is the past.** You experienced trauma as a child, and you felt very unsafe. But you can find ways to accept that you are safe now. Look around, observe where you are, and tell yourself that you are in the present; you are not in your trauma anymore.

→ **Ask your therapist about coping with residual trauma responses or PTSD.** A therapist can help you practice deep, slow breathing exercises and work out strategies to get you out of the past and back into the present.

Rebuild Your Self-Esteem

Self-esteem is the overall sense of self-worth or self-respect a person feels. A daughter whose mother is narcissistic has not typically had any nurturing or validation that helps her to recognize her value. As the daughter, you have likely focused all of your energy and attention on your narcissistic mother, leaving you no time or support to explore who you are, what is important to you, and your inherent value. You haven't learned to love yourself. Furthermore, living in your mother's shadow and hearing her criticism deeply damaged your self-esteem. You may see yourself in a very negative light. Thankfully, we can correct this, and you have already started this part of your recovery.

→ **Practice loving and respecting yourself.** Setting boundaries is one way to start this process because we protect what we value. Boundaries are a way of empowering yourself. Setting a boundary is an act of self-care. This is the foundation from which to build your self-esteem.

→ **Trust yourself.** Your body is giving you messages constantly, and it's time for you to start listening. Luckily, our intuition or gut reaction doesn't turn off, even when we've been shut down and neglected. My guess is that your gut has been trying to get you to notice it from day one, but you have not been able to heed it. You get to follow your intuition now. You know what is best for you and what is not.

→ **Focus on the facts.** A narcissist manipulated you for years, spinning lies about what kind of person you are. But your mother doesn't control reality. You may be stuck in a pattern of negative self-talk, but what if you really examine the neutral facts of who you are as a person? Take some time to think about your accomplishments, big or small: Maybe you got a bachelor's degree, or maybe you trapped a spider in a jar and released it outside your home instead of killing it. You have accomplishments, and you are a worthy person. You may even find it helpful to write down some neutral facts about yourself, without making a value judgment. Read these facts aloud to yourself. Do the facts align with your sense of self-worth?

It's time to shift your focus to yourself and what you need in order to heal and thrive. Focusing on yourself does not mean that you are narcissistic. It's simply time to care for your wounds. This is the time for you to slow down, not be in survival mode, and not be hypervigilant. This is the time for you to pay attention and be mindful. Really take in what is happening around you and study your reactions. This is how you learn who you are, what's important to you, and how much value you actually have.

Daily Affirmations

There is a phrase often used in recovery, "fake it till you make it," which means to act as if you are already thinking, believing, and doing what you have set out to think, believe, and do. When you start the practice of daily affirmations, it may feel foreign or awkward to say nice things to yourself. But if you fake it till you make it, this practice will feel more natural. You will start to consider that the kind words coming from your mouth might actually be true.

It is incredibly important to push your way through the awkwardness and say something nice to yourself, to tell that little girl who lives inside of you how important and strong she is and always has been. I often encourage my clients to write words of affirmation on their bathroom mirrors so that they are one of the first things they see in the morning.

The mean things you say to yourself are likely the messages you received as a child that you are repeating now. When you notice that you have called yourself dumb, stop in your tracks and notice the unkindness of your words. Take a moment to contradict them. It's time to start this practice, and I encourage you to say at least five kind things to yourself every day.

Some simple examples are:

→ I matter.
→ I am proud of myself.
→ I deserve love.
→ I am brave and strong.
→ I am doing my best.

The most important words to say to yourself are the ones you believe, so use these examples as a starting point and add your own.

Wall of Protection

In order to protect yourself and perhaps your own family, you must value and love yourself. Your own interests and needs should take top priority as you proceed down the path of recovering and growing. This is going to feel weird because it is something you have not yet done for yourself. You grew up with your mother's extreme self-centeredness as an example. As an adult, you may worry that you are behaving in a narcissistic way when you start to practice protecting yourself, but once you start this practice, you will not want to look back. We're not talking about super-ficial "self-care" like shopping sprees or extravagant trips. We're talking about following your intuition, removing yourself from damaging relationships, and saying no to demands from others that feel harmful to you. You are worthy of your own love and care. Here, we'll go over some strategies for keeping yourself safe.

Protecting Yourself

As you have probably guessed, protecting yourself involves setting boundaries, so you're already well on your way in this process. While it is exhausting to interact with your narcissist, you may not expect how exhausting it will be to stand up for yourself. Your mother is used to getting her way and being able to manipulate you. When you stop this cycle, she is going to raise the stakes. This is to be expected when changing any behavior, and her intense reaction will pass.

In psychological terms, we are talking about classical conditioning through positive and negative reinforcements. If you are on the phone with your mother and she crosses a boundary, you simply tell her that she has crossed your boundary and end the call. This is negative reinforcement as you are taking something she wants—your time and attention—away from her. If she respects your boundaries, you reward that behavior with positive reinforcement. Let's say you told her she can't accuse you of not loving her when you have to cancel a weekday lunch. Then, when you have to cancel a weekday lunch, she respects the boundary by being polite about it. You would say something like, "I appreciate you understanding that I can't have lunch with you today, and I would like a raincheck." This reinforces her respect of your limits and rewards her by giving her your time and attention when you are able.

As you commit to this process, you also need to positively reinforce this new behavior in yourself by showing yourself kindness when you have enforced your boundaries. This means practicing affirmations, giving yourself alone time to emotionally recharge, and reminding yourself that you deserve peace and respect.

Protecting Your Family

You may have noticed your mother trying to manipulate your children, partner, or other people close to you. This is typical narcissistic behavior, but it can be easily missed because it is manipulation that you are not experiencing directly. You may see that your mother is texting your husband to ask how you're doing because she is unable to reach you directly. Your mother can't stand the loss of power she is starting to feel with you and will try other avenues to maintain it.

It gets really sticky when it comes to your children. Certainly the children should be able to spend time with grandma, shouldn't they? The answer is no, not if grandma is using them to get to you or, equally likely, using them as a source to supply her narcissistic needs.

Protecting people you love might come a bit more naturally to you than protecting yourself. Use that to your advantage. The boundaries you put in place for yourself are certainly the same boundaries you should have for your children and loved ones. This means that you need to tell people close to you why you are trying to shield them from the destructive behavior of your mother. You may have to explain in some detail, as even your partner may not understand the level of emotional abuse you have experienced. Ultimately, with some communication to your loved ones about the protective wall you are establishing, you should have their support.

You Are Not Your Mother

Many daughters of narcissistic mothers who come to my practice for therapy worry that they might also be narcissists. However, your concern about being a narcissist is a huge indicator that you are likely not one. Narcissists don't typically come to therapy asking for help, nor will they admit that their behavior is out of the ordinary. As the daughter of the narcissistic mother, you are likely to share some traits with her because she raised you to think and behave as she does. She modeled adulthood for you from the start, and you didn't realize her model was unhealthy until you were old enough to have relationships outside of your childhood home. When you formed relationships with people outside the home, you observed that others can actually behave kindly and unselfishly. As you read this book, you are likely recognizing the level to which you are not like your mother.

Another interesting phenomenon that I have experienced in my therapy practice is the number of women who have felt like the black sheep of their family. These daughters of narcissistic mothers are trying to break a chain of emotional abuse that has likely occurred for generations. If they have chosen not to engage on their mothers's terms, they are accused of acting out of the norm. If that's what being the black sheep is, wear it like a crown. Embrace that label and be proud of the courage it took not to follow in your mother's footsteps or enable her behavior. This will help you on your path to finding yourself. If you do find yourself being judgmental or selfish, take a moment to challenge your own thoughts in order to change your reactions. We are bound to see traits of our parents show up in our own behaviors, both good and bad. When these behaviors are what you recognize as narcissistic traits from your mother, pay attention to what you were feeling that led to your actions. You can interrupt the cycle. You are already taking a step in that direction just by reading this book.

Mothering Yourself

You can give that little girl who still lives inside of you the gift of a healthy, loving, and nurturing presence. Mothering your inner child is possible no matter your current age, and it is essential. Once you get in touch with that inner child, you will start to clearly see the pain that has lived inside of you, and you will start to see a path forward. As a child, you didn't get the love and support you needed, and getting in touch with that inner child will help you return to those painful memories and comfort and love that version of yourself. Sit with your inner child as she grieves the loneliness and lack of care, and contrast that with love and acceptance.

Nurture Yourself

You likely did not receive the nurturing you needed as a baby or young child to feel securely attached to your mother. When things went awry, your mother didn't comfort you. She may have dismissed your pain and made you feel insignificant. She did not praise you when you got that part in the school play or celebrate with you when you won the spelling bee. She may have, in contrast, said something like "you stuttered when you spelled that last word" or "why didn't you get the *lead* role in the play," disregarding the courage and effort you put into these accomplishments.

Luckily, nurturing your efforts and praising your accomplishments is something you can do for your present-day self and your inner child. You can look at a picture of yourself as a little girl and talk to her, tell her how proud you are of her for making it through such a rough childhood. Tell her how impressed you are with her ability to function when she was in school despite having to go play that softball game with no one cheering in the stands for her. Help her understand why she felt sad and lonely most of the time, and let her know that she deserved more. Affirm that you won't allow her to get pushed to the side again. You will start to heal your pain by comforting your inner child and allowing her a safe place to feel her emotions.

Be Your Own Cheerleader

Once you've gotten comfortable with the idea of nurturing yourself, your next step is to cheer your current self on. You didn't get this kind of encouragement from your mother, but now you get to be your own cheerleader. Daughters of narcissistic mothers are used to being pushed to the side, quietly accomplishing their goals with little to no recognition. Now is your time to change that. Celebrate everything you want to celebrate—the big, the small, and the in-between.

Since you are probably quite used to letting accomplishments go unnoticed by others, celebrating and cheering for yourself may feel self-indulgent and awkward. Nonetheless, give it a try. Being your own cheerleader is incredibly important to your sense of self and the continued development of your identity. You can start small. Perhaps you can do a happy dance for getting all the laundry folded when you really just wanted to take a nap. You can buy yourself a gift for getting a promotion. Celebrate yourself to whatever degree you would like.

When you doubt yourself, remind yourself how intelligent, loving, empathetic, and bright you are. Pat yourself on the back once you have achieved your goal, and tell yourself what a great achievement it was. Take yourself out to a celebratory dinner when you have done something you are proud of, or reach out to a friend or loved one to share your good news. You deserve the attention and praise that you receive when you start to recognize your value and worth. Cheering yourself on is another way of nurturing and loving yourself, and it is long overdue.

Mother Yourself

We need our mothers to nurture us. We also need them to teach us how to love ourselves, forgive ourselves, navigate the world around us, and figure out who we are. A narcissistic mother is not capable of this. As a result, you have likely developed some unhealthy coping skills to manage the pain you experience from not receiving the mothering you need. This lack of mothering may have left you with shame in who you are and a feeling of being unworthy. Mothering yourself can help you heal. You can identify what it means to be a nurturing, loving, warm, and affectionate mother. As you mother yourself, you will start to more clearly understand your own needs.

When you see traits in mothers that resonate with you, explore them and mimic them toward your inner child. These role-model mothers could be people you know, or even characters in books or movies.

Here are some things you can start to say to yourself:

→ Being in a bad mood does not mean that you are a bad person.

→ Our emotions do not define who we are. It is safe to feel your feelings because they will pass.

→ You can make mistakes and still be worthy of love.

→ You can be proud of yourself without being narcissistic. You are not like the narcissistic mother who raised you.

→ You do not have to rely on any ineffective coping skills you developed to avoid pain. You are an adult, you are in control now, and you are keeping yourself safe.

→ You can be who you are, and you can thrive now.

Your Support Team

Many of the women who come to my practice do not have an emotional support team to help them through their recovery process. This is not unusual. Growing up with a narcissistic mother, you likely learned to fend for yourself. You may have trouble trusting others enough to let them support you. As you learn to build your emotional protection in the right places, it'll be important to let your guard down and allow people support you. Try seeking out emotionally healthy relatives, friends, a faith community, a therapist, or trauma support groups, to name a few.

Having support around you will help you immeasurably as you work toward recovery. Empower yourself to move past the discomfort you will feel in asking others for help. Try to move past the feeling that you are burdening others—that will only keep you isolated. When you've identified who is supportive to you, take the leap and call them when you're feeling low or need someone to confirm that you are on the right track. You deserve someone to talk to about your fears and sadness as well as your successes. A friend will validate your experience, and validation is something every daughter of a narcissistic mother really needs. Knowing that you have people in your corner helps you feel loved and accepted, which also helps you remember that you are worthy.

Amanda Navigates No Contact

Amanda first sought therapy after being blamed by her father for being the "emotional" one in the family. She thought her father was narcissistic and had done a substantial amount of research on narcissism before seeking therapy. She saw her father as being controlling and manipulative, and she felt she needed skills to manage her relationship with him. As we worked together, Amanda's perspective on her father began to change. She started to realize that his demands were actually the demands of her mother. Her father was not the narcissist, but the enabler. She could now see how he acted as her mother's flying monkey, and she saw that her sister was her mother's "golden child" while Amanda was the "scapegoat," roles that are common in narcissistic families.

As time passed and Amanda started to identify and understand her family's dynamics, she saw that her peace had to come from within. Because of their toxic patterns, she was not able to rely on anyone in her large family of origin to support her. Through therapy, she started to understand the importance of nurturing and mothering herself, and she embraced the challenge of re-mothering herself. She followed the steps and tools that have been outlined in this book and worked her way through intense exercises to get in touch with her inner child throughout her girlhood.

Amanda was flexible and curious enough to follow the different paths her recovery journey took her on. She got stuck on her toddlerhood and could not move forward for several weeks until she talked through her feelings in therapy. This roadblock was a manifestation of not having the words, as a toddler, to express how she was feeling. After Amanda recognized this, she was able to speak to what that baby version of herself could not describe—fear—and ultimately move on to other stages of development.

When she reached the apex of her journey, Amanda envisioned all of the versions of herself meeting on a beach in Hawaii where they came together under her loving embrace. She felt complete, as she had nurtured each version of herself at each developmental stage of her life. She provided her selves with love and unconditional acceptance. At each stage of childhood, she allowed herself the time needed to heal herself before moving on. As you can imagine, this took several months, a lot of tears, and a lot of laughter. Amanda worked through it. She focused on the love and support she created in her life, and she learned that she mattered.

CHAPTER FIVE REVIEW

Throughout this chapter we have focused on understanding accurate terms used to identify your experiences: trauma, neglect, and abuse. You have survived, and you are now learning skills to figure out who you are and how to protect the person you are becoming. Understanding that you have experienced complex trauma is a huge step to take because if you don't label your experience correctly, you are invalidating your experience and perpetuating the neglect from your past. Acknowledging the truth is an act of self-care. This validation opens the door to building yourself up and loving yourself. Here's what I hope you'll take from this chapter:

→ You experienced trauma in the form of emotional neglect. You may have experienced other forms of trauma as well.

→ You never had the opportunity to build a firm sense of self, much less self-esteem.

→ You saw yourself as a person who could never be good enough for your mother.

→ Despite any similarities, you are not your mother. You have empathy, love, and kindness within you.

→ You have the power to be the nurturing caregiver that you have always needed. That little neglected girl still lives within you, and she is waiting for your love and attention.

→ There are people you can count on. You can build your support network and rely on their love and encouragement as you walk this path.

CHAPTER SIX

Taking Care of You

When therapists stress the importance of self-care, it is not our intent for you to indulge in bubble baths and spa days (although sometimes these are great ways to practice self-care). Rather, we want to know if you had a full night's sleep, if you drank enough water, if you've been nourishing yourself with healthy foods and eating regularly. We want to know if you have taken the time to shower and wear clean clothes, if you have brushed your teeth and washed your face.

As someone who has been abused and neglected, you may not always realize the importance of basic self-care, including basic hygiene. Being raised by a narcissist, you learned to put your needs second. It is critical that you are caring for yourself day-to-day. The act of caring for yourself, even if you're feeling low, is a demonstration that you are worthy of love. Self-care will help you maintain your mental health, and it will also help you build up your self-esteem and sense of self. Let's make sure you're covering the basics first.

Vitality of Self-Care

When you have a steady routine of caring for yourself, it creates more stability in your mental health. As you recover from narcissistic abuse and neglect, it is important to escape the mindset that you must take care of others before you attend to your own needs. You have been putting yourself last throughout your childhood and into adulthood because this behavior was expected by your mother. Her needs always came first. It is finally your turn to know what it feels like to be cared for.

Now is the time for self-reflection. Notice what your body is telling you it needs; nourish your mind with love and acceptance. As you practice these skills, they will become a way of life, and you will learn what it feels like to love yourself and reject what feels wrong. Pay more attention to your intuition. We all have it, and it is one of our best guides.

In my practice, I have seen many daughters of narcissistic mothers be quite fearful of getting into another narcissistic relationship or falling back into old patterns with their mothers. My advice is this:

→ Always trust your gut.
→ Pay attention to red flags.
→ Don't make excuses for another person's behavior.
→ Accept that there are people who don't have the qualities that you appreciate and need to see in others.
→ Reject anyone or anything that feels unstable or dangerous.

The ability to get in tune with yourself takes practice. Freedom from hypervigilance and worry will allow you to be in touch with your intuition.

A deeper level of self-care is connecting with others. We've discussed the importance of a support network.

At our core, we are social animals who need connection with one another.

Stay connected to whatever makes you feel most at peace. That could mean things like spending time in nature or in your house of worship. Exercise is another vital piece of self-care. Movement helps you be in touch with your body and understand where you hold stress and trauma.

MEDITATION AND SELF-CARE

Meditation is a really great place to start the exploration of self-care because it is quiet and self-centering. Meditation doesn't have to happen while you're sitting on the floor in a quiet place with your eyes closed; you can choose to sit in your favorite chair or lie down under a pretty tree, or wherever feels comfortable to you. Focus on your breath, or the sensations in your body. Take time to really pay attention to the feeling in your toes, and then draw your attention up slowly through the rest of your body. If you choose, you can have an affirming mantra that you repeat. If your mind wanders, pause, take note of the distraction, and then bring your focus back to the moment you're in.

Meditation can be particularly helpful for people who experience trauma-related symptoms, because meditating is all about being present in your body. When you experience trauma, you can get repeatedly snagged in your past experiences. But through meditation, you bring your attention back to yourself and your current surroundings. The skills you learn while meditating, even if you only meditate for short periods of time, can help you re-center yourself when you get upset.

Release Control and Practice Acceptance

The practice of acceptance is life-changing. As with the grief cycle, acceptance is a difficult place to reach, and we may fight ourselves in getting there because it can be misinterpreted as giving up or surrendering. However, accepting reality is one of the bravest things you can do for yourself. When you can stop bargaining and wishing that your past was different, you free yourself. You will no longer live in a world of "if only," and you'll get to start building the life that you want for yourself.

Surely you have recognized times when you may have thought, "If only I got better grades, if only I were better at ballet, if only I were better at *something*, my mother would have spent more time with me." You might have had a more realistic way of thinking: "If only she were kinder, if only she weren't my mother, if only neighbor Suzy were my mother ... " When you do this, you are not accepting the truth of your situation, and you will remain stuck.

You need to radically accept the truth of your present and your past and stop living in the "if only" zone. It is only through an authentic life that you can create a better future for yourself. Your mother probably set high standards for living. You have learned that having designer clothes or living in the best neighborhood will make you happy, but is this true? Part of releasing control means not wishing for what you don't or didn't have. When you release control, instead you appreciate what you do have. Things like sunny days, beautiful flowers, or a favorite pair of pajamas can be a source of joy. These little things can make a huge difference, and cultivating acceptance is so much more positive than spinning your wheels trying to create a perfect past that never existed.

Take a mental inventory of what already exists in your life that is fulfilling (you may even want to write a list). This accounting will help you make the switch from control to acceptance. When you learn to appreciate what comes to you easily or freely, you can let go of things that don't matter. When you appreciate how good it feels to talk to a friend who truly loves you for *you*, you won't need to keep avoiding the truth of your past. Instead, you will be drawn to fully living and experiencing your present.

The Illusion of Control

The abuse and neglect you experienced leads you to try to exert a huge amount of control in your life. You likely overcompensate in order to make up for the lack of control you had as a child. But you can only control yourself and your own responses; trying to control anything outside of yourself is a futile effort. No matter how hard you try, the amount of control you have over outside forces is very limited, and you have virtually no control over the actions of others. The illusion of control is inviting and can even be irresistible, but once you realize it really is an illusion, you will feel freer.

Letting go of the illusion of control means practicing acceptance. This will clear up space in your mind, and you can then use that energy for something else. The energy can be used to mindfully explore what it really is that you need in order to heal.

What stops many of us from giving up control is that we are holding onto unrealistic expectations. You wish that things had been different or fair; you wish you could have justice for the wrongs of the past. Accepting reality and letting go of your expectations will be the key to contentment.

Create Goals for Your Life

During this process, you have probably thought of some goals to get you to a point where you are no longer affected by the pain and suffering you've experienced. As you do the work described in this book, you are going to be in a position to meet your goals. Goals will keep you moving through your recovery process and give you a foundation from which to continue to figure out who you are. You need to focus on where you want your life to go, and who you want to be in it. Setting goals will keep you going in the right direction, and it will keep you from getting stuck in the cycle of grief and wishing things had been different. You are in a position now to keep looking toward the future and having it unfold on your terms. You are not going to live under the control of a mother who expects you to behave or dress how she wants and adore her without consideration that you are your own person.

Goals that you choose to pursue need to really resonate with you on a deep level, otherwise you won't see the value in following through. Here are some goals to consider, and to use as a jumping-off point for setting goals that are important to you:

→ **Remove any behaviors or ways of thinking that do not feel genuine.** What this means is, if you are used to saying *yes* to every request that comes your way in order to keep the peace, allow yourself permission to say *no*. Give yourself permission to take time to consider a request you feel unsure about.

→ **Take time to figure out what you believe in and what is important to you.** When others express their opinions, notice what your true inner reaction is. Take time to tease it apart and land on a position that sits well with you and feels genuine to you. Notice what that feels like in your mind and your body. When you land on thoughts and opinions that are truly your own, there should be a feeling of comfort and certainty.

→ **Trust your wisdom.** Throughout your life with your mother, you have acquiesced to her authority and decision-making. As a result, you have not learned to trust yourself. Now is the time to change that way of thinking. Start to take opportunities to make decisions big or small. When they turn out to be right, celebrate in that. If they were wrong, welcome that experience as a learning opportunity.

Melinda Feels Empowered

As you have seen throughout this book, going back to care for the child who is still a part of you with love, affection, and nurturing is a key component to recovering. You can create a healthier attachment style by doing inner child work as my client Melinda did.

Inner child work is a mode of treatment we use in my practice, and Melinda used it to help her reach her goals of feeling whole and confident in her choices. Previously, she spent time trying to heal her relationship with her mother by acquiescing to her demands. She only saw her mother face-to-face a few times a year due to distance, so she thought it was sustainable to continue in this dynamic. Not long ago, Melinda was having work done on her house and she decided she was not going to go out of her way to plan her mother's upcoming visit in tedious detail. Previously, Melinda would go through her house with a fine-tooth comb, hide new purchases, and make sure every nook and cranny was spotless.

Melinda thought that she had set boundaries with her mother. But with the visit looming, she realized that she had simply avoided regular phone conversations with her mother and then tolerated her behaviors when they were together. When Melinda decided that she was no longer interested in meeting her mother's expectations, she decided it was time to work on her goal of being her authentic self—flaws and all—with her mother.

Melinda took steps to trust herself. She agonized about buying new furniture for her living room because she knew if she did, she would have to answer her mother's questions about why she spent money. Through setting goals to stop and take a look at who she was trusting to control her life, Melinda decided it was time to trust herself. She made the decision to buy the furniture, and she committed to telling her mother only that the old furniture needed to be replaced. She would not give her mother any further explanation. Melinda worked up to the goal with small steps, such as choosing to trust her judgment for the repairs done on her house. She listened to her intuition and her own desires. She validated those choices, which is something she did not experience as a child. By the time her mother arrived, Melinda was proud of what she had accomplished in repairing and furnishing her home on her own. She did not make any excuses or apologies, and she is now more confident in decision-making overall.

There has been a lot of research on how to reach goals effectively. The research shows that smaller, more attainable goals are most effective. When we create big, overarching goals without smaller objectives or steps to reach them, we are likely to give up on the large goal because it can feel over-whelming. For example, if your goal is to behave in a way that will garner respect from your mother, you will need to start by setting boundaries. Enforcing these boundaries is a step to reaching the larger goal of receiving her respect. If you simply say to her, "I will not allow you to disrespect me any longer," how do you achieve that? The larger goal is receiving respect, so the objective is to set expectations of what you will accept from her and what you will not. You will achieve that goal through expressing your boundaries and then con-sistently reinforcing those boundaries with concrete actions that you plan in advance. Another goal can be trusting your intuition. When something does not feel right, make it part of your interventions to take a step back and explore what you are feeling, then move forward cautiously.

Seeking Professional Help

There is more understanding and acceptance of mental health care than ever, but we still have some work to do to completely remove the stigma. There is no shame in seeking professional help, and we may need to do so several times throughout our lives. Narcissistic abuse happens under the radar and is often difficult for the victim to even describe. It is hard to explain to your friends how devastated you felt when your mother criticized your makeup. You cannot fully explain the deeper meaning in that criticism.

A therapist will understand the tricky nuances of that criticism and help you see how this kind of criticism seeps into your psyche. While there is not an abundance of therapists who specialize in treating victims of narcissistic abuse, most therapists understand narcissism and how it contributes to emotional abuse. Another benefit to seeking a therapist's help is that it can show you what a healthy relationship looks like. While your relationship with your therapist is a professional one, there is also a personal connection, as you will have to learn to trust your therapist in order to share your pain and allow them to support you. Through your relationship with your therapist, you can get support, reinforcement, and encouragement for the changes you are making.

There are several books written by professionals that can continue to help you on your journey, such as this one. You may also choose to seek out support groups either in person or online. There are some social media groups to help survivors of narcissistic abuse support each other.

However, these alternative resources are not a replacement for professional therapy. The fact that books, therapists, and groups exist around this topic can be validating. You'll clearly see that you are not alone and that other women have had similar experiences with narcissistic mothers. The damage wrought by a narcissistic mother plays a role in how you interact with your romantic partners, your coworkers, the grocery clerk, the babysitter, and your own children. Therapy can help you learn to trust that you are moving in the right direction, and help you get back on track when you have lost focus.

With a therapist, you can practice how to converse with your mother by role-playing. You can just check in with them to normalize what you are feeling and experiencing. A well-trained therapist will know the correct way to support you on your journey. Recovering takes work, and there is no reason to take this on by yourself. Please seek and accept the help that is available around you and start living the life you have dreamed of living.

CHAPTER SIX REVIEW

Throughout this chapter you have seen how important taking care of yourself is to recovering. Showing yourself love and acceptance is a necessity and not to be considered selfish or weak. These concepts will be foreign to you as you start working on them, but you will become used to feeling valued and worthy. The message you have gotten from your mother is that you exist for her needs, but now you understand that her expectations were unacceptable. You are justified in believing that you deserve love, kindness, and respect, and you now have some tools to help you toward this goal.

My hope is that you will release abusive and toxic people from your life no matter who they are, even if the toxic person is your own mother. It is okay for you to surround yourself with supportive, loving people and create your own family and support system. Finally, there is no shame in seeking support from a therapist, a spiritual leader, a peer group, or an agency that helps with domestic abuse.

Important takeaways from this chapter are:

→ You need to practice self-care.
→ Control is not as important as it may seem.
→ Accepting things for what they are is liberating.
→ Setting goals will keep you focused.
→ Therapy will be an important tool in living your best life.

A Final Word

Congratulations! You are on your way to creating a life filled with confidence, trust, love, and acceptance. It takes considerable effort to recognize narcissistic abuse, and it takes even more effort to accept that this is the relationship you have experienced with your mother. By reading this book, you have already started the process of radically accepting things for what they are, which is possibly the biggest step toward good mental health.

This book is only one of many tools that will help you along through your growth and recovery process. As you continue to work on yourself, please refer back to what you have learned in the book in order to reinforce the steps you are taking to heal from the abuse of your narcissistic mother. Keep in mind that there are others who understand what you have experienced and they can support you. Seek out those people and build safe relationships. Trust your gut, always! That's where your intuition lives, and when you start paying attention to it, you will find that it is not likely to fail you.

Your body sends you other messages, too, and you can work with a therapist to help you understand these messages. If you are feeling overwhelmed, listen when your body tells you that you may need to take a seat for a while to recharge. Allow yourself the freedom to take a nap when needed: you are healing wounds, and rest will help you do so successfully. Remember that it's perfectly acceptable to put your own needs first. In fact, sometimes you must put yourself first so that you will have the capacity to meet the needs of others if you choose. Put boundaries in place without feeling guilty and remind yourself that healthy relationships thrive with good boundaries.

Please remember that it is perfectly acceptable to say *no* to requests that are not appealing to you or otherwise raise red flags. Trust your gut when you want to decline an invitation or request. Be mindful, focus on all the magnificent things present in your life, be grateful for them, and do things that make you happy. Gratitude changes your perspective and will help you recognize and take pride in all of the hard work you have done and continue to do. Engage socially to the extent that you are comfortable, because even the most introverted of us need connection with others. Positive friendships will help replace the negative feelings you have experienced in your relationship with your mother.

You have taken on the challenge of recovering and becoming the person you want to be. It's no small task, but it may be one of the most rewarding journeys of your life, so keep going even when you feel like it is impossible. Most of all, remember you can do this!

Resources

The Narcissistic Abuse Recovery Center
NarcAbuseRecoveryCenter.com

Stephens Therapy Associates
StephensTherapy.com

VAWnet
A clearinghouse of domestic violence information compiled by the National Resource Center on Domestic Violence.
VAWnet.org

The National Domestic Violence Hotline
TheHotline.org

References

American Psychiatric Association. *Diagnostic and Statistical Manual of Mental Disorders,* 5th ed. Arlington, VA: American Psychiatric Association, 2013.

Harvard Health Publications. "Not Getting Over It: Post-Traumatic Stress Disorder." Last modified March 2014. Health.Harvard.edu/newsletter_article/Not _getting_over_it_Post-traumatic_stress_disorder.

Jankowiak-Siuda, Kamila and Wojciech Zajkowski. "A Neural Model of Mechanisms of Empathy Deficits in Narcissism." *Medical Science Monitor* 19 (November 2013): 934–941. doi: 10.12659/MSM.889593.

Lee, Louise. "Focus on Small Steps First, Then Shift to the Larger Goal." *Insights by Stanford Business.* May 17, 2017. GSB.Stanford.edu/insights/focus-small-steps -first-then-shift-larger-goal.

Linehan, Marsha M. *DBT Skills Training Handouts and Worksheets.* New York: Guilford Press, 2015.

National Center for PTSD. "Self-Help and Coping." Accessed May 17, 2020. PTSD.VA.gov/gethelp/selfhelp _coping.asp.

Stinson, Frederick S., Deborah A. Dawson, Rise B. Goldstein, S. Patricia Chou, Boji Huang, Sharon M. Smith, W. June Ruan, et al. "Prevalence, Correlates, Disability, and Comorbidity of DSM-IV Narcissistic Personality Disorder: Results from the Wave 2 National Epidemiologic Survey on Alcohol and Related Conditions." *The Journal of Clinical Psychiatry* 69, no. 7 (2008): 1033–45. doi:10.4088/jcp.v69n0701.

Index

About the Author

 **Brenda Stephens** is a Licensed Professional Clinical Counselor who works solely with survivors of narcissistic abuse and trauma. She obtained her education through the University of Wisconsin system and is a board member for CALPCC, the professional organization for clinical counselors in the state of California. Brenda is the founder of a group practice in Southern California and a coaching practice, the Narcissistic Abuse Recovery Center, assisting survivors of narcissistic abuse globally. She offers training to other therapists to help them support their clients who are children, partners, and others who have been abused by a person, or persons, with narcissistic traits.